Dishes
&
DOMINION

*How Christian Housewives
Can Change the World*

Leah D. Smith

AMERICAN VISION, INC.
POWDER SPRINGS, GEORGIA

Diapers, Dishes & **DOMINION** by Leah D. Smith

Copyright © 2011 by Leah D. Smith. All rights reserved.

No part of this publication may be reproduced, stored in a retrieval system, or transmitted in any form by any means, electronic, mechanical, photocopy, recording, or otherwise, without the prior, written permission of the publisher, except for brief quotations in critical reviews or articles.

Published by:

    American Vision, Inc.
    3150-A Florence Road
    Powder Springs, GA 30127–5385

    www.AmericanVision.org
    1-800-628-9460

Scripture quotations from the Holy Bible, *New American Standard Version* © 1960, 1962, 1963, 1968, 1971, 1972, 1973, 1975, 1995 by The Lockman Foundation. Used by permission.

Scripture quotations from the Holy Bible, *New International Version* © 1973, 1978, 1984, 2011 by Biblica, Inc. Used by permission. All rights reserved worldwide.

Scripture quotations from the Holy Bible, *New Living Translation* © 1996, 2004, 2007 by Tyndale House Foundation. Used by permission of Tyndale House Publishers, Inc., Carol Stream, Illinois 60188. All rights reserved.

Scripture quotations from the Holy Bible, *English Standard Version* © 2001 by Crossway, a publishing ministry of Good News Publishers. Used by permission. All rights reserved.

Typeset by Michael Minkoff, Jr.
Front Cover Design by Joseph Malleck at Malleck Design: http://www.MalleckDesign.com
Back Cover Photo by Revival Arts Studio: http://RevivalArtsStudio.com
Cover Layout by Luis Lovelace

ISBN: 978-1-936577-18-7

CONTENTS

FOREWORD *by* Carol DeMar	VII
PREFACE	IX
CHAPTER 1: *Doom, Gloom, a Mop & a Broom*	1
CHAPTER 2: *Spirals & Ghosts*	7
CHAPTER 3: *Dominoes of Destiny*	15
CHAPTER 4: *How To Be a Queen*	23
CHAPTER 5: *Rugrat-Loosed and Fancy-Free*	29
CHAPTER 6: *Pills & Bifocals*	37
CHAPTER 7: *God's Law for ~~Dummies~~ Mommies*	45
CHAPTER 8: *The Idle Mind is Whose Playground?*	51
CHAPTER 9: *Pabulum… Yum?*	61
CHAPTER 10: *Politics, Schmolitics*	75
CHAPTER 11: *Left Wing, Right Wing… Am I a Chicken?*	85
CHAPTER 12: *Casseroles, Presidents & Pedicures*	91
CHAPTER 13: *The Whole Lump of ~~Carbs~~ Dough*	105
CHAPTER 14: *The End is Near… or Far?*	115
CHAPTER 15: *Whence, Whither, Hither, and To Whom?*	127
CHAPTER 16: *Return to Eden*	135
CHAPTER 17: *Seven Questions*	147
CHAPTER 18: *The Ultimate Legacy*	153
CONCLUSION: *I Found the Puzzle Box!*	163
ENDNOTES	167
FURTHER READING	171
CONNECT WITH THE AUTHOR	175

FOREWORD

s I was reading about Leah Smith's journey from fear-ridden, rebellious teen to courageous, self-governing adult, I realized that the anxiety that once crippled her still afflicts many of today's young people—even those that claim to be Christians.

Thanks to both a blessed upbringing and a wonderful marriage to a strong, Reformed husband, I have believed the theology that Leah shares with her readers for most of my life. The majority of today's Christians, however, have not had that privilege, so their already present apprehensions about the future are aggravated, and often distorted, by everything from dangerously incorrect end times "prophecies" to government policies which jeopardize the stability of our nation and the well-being of tomorrow's families. While our culture continues to endorse increasingly deviant behavior, regardless of the consequences, and radical environmentalists bellow predictions about the total destruction of "Mother Nature," Christians either hole up behind their church walls of presumed safety—never engaging the world—or we become *of* the world in a vain attempt at cultural relevance. Both approaches ignore God's Word, especially those passages written specifically to help believers wage war on the present powers of darkness and overcome the real challenges of our time.

Every generation has had to deal with fear. My generation worried that friends and family members being sent off to war in Vietnam would never return. Fear can paralyze us when we permit it to control our minds and steal our joy. Leah recounts her passage from fear into freedom—from an anxious rebel to a Christian wife and mother who learned to trust the Lord in all things. She was once afraid to have children because she believed the world could end at any time, and she did not want them to suffer through the "Tribulation." As she studied the Scriptures on her own, she realized that many of her fears were a result of her own misunderstandings. How many of us have wholeheartedly believed the words of others—whether from a pastor, friend, or parent—without verifying the facts? Look at the confusion that ensues when, failing to fact-check the claims contained in a chain e-mail, we unwittingly prolong the lifespan of misinformation by forwarding it to all our friends and family. Most of the time, those e-mails are bogus, and so are most popular conceptions of God's Word. We should never blindly accept someone else's interpretation of the Bible—we should be willing to study it diligently for ourselves.

Leah furnishes a vault full of valuable information for young women. Regardless of what our culture attempts to tell us, the family—a father and mother with children—is crucial to a healthy society and its future because that is the way God ordained it. A godly mother exercising her faith through her understanding of God's truth has a mighty impact on her husband and children, and even on her nation. We always hear that children are our future. What will our future hold if our children do not embrace the truth? And how will they embrace the truth if they have not heard it… if their minds have not been steeped in God's Word? We are already reaping what we have sown. Mothers have not served the Lord Jesus Christ, and they have raised children who despise the Creator and His Law. The picture is not yet complete, but, even now, it is clear that we are putting the finishing brush-strokes on our own destruction.

The tide must turn, but that will not happen unless Christian parents begin again to model Christ biblically for their children. Leah Smith's *Diapers, Dishes & Dominion* will encourage other young wives and mothers who have fears and insecurities about life. Leah's own life began to turn around when her heart comprehended this verse from John 8:32: *Then you will know the truth, and the truth will set you free.* I pray her book will be a blessing to those who read it. May God use it to help set other women free from their fears, so they can be used powerfully to further His kingdom.

–Carol DeMar

PREFACE

am not a theologian. I am not an expert of any kind. I am simply a wife and a stay-at-home mom. I have written this for myself as a record of my journey thus far, of everything I have learned in the last three years, and as reminder of where I am going when it feels like times are bleak.

I also write this for my children. Should anything happen to me, they would not know first-hand all my thoughts and convictions on these matters. I hope to pass down any wisdom acquired and lessons learned to my grandchildren and beyond.

Lastly, I write this for any wife or mother who wishes to understand her significance in history—how one life can alter the course of paths and set patterns for generations. I write it for anyone who wishes to gain insight into why changing diapers and doing dishes are more than just "the hardest job on earth." In the Kingdom of God, the home is the training ground from where both warriors and noble princesses emerge—or do not.

I do not have all the answers, but I know the One who does. He has already given us a Book full of them, containing all we need for every aspect of life.

CHAPTER 1

Doom, Gloom, a Mop & a Broom

THE END IS NEAR. I'm tired of hearing it. Maybe you're tired of hearing it too. Christian bookstores dedicate entire sections to novels and prophecy books predicting the end of the world and the imminent return of Jesus. They tell us to hang on tight because the Rapture might happen any minute. In the meantime, the same authors keep writing more books and making more money. Eventually, one has to ask the question: what do these authors plan on doing with all this money and fame after the Rapture happens? To whom will they leave that inheritance?

While this is happening and everyone is waiting for Jesus to come back, stay-at-home-moms are mopping and sweeping the kitchen floors, cleaning up the baby powder that someone dumped out all over the living room, and making casseroles. For some of us, a looming—yet sometimes unconscious—question remains on the back burner of our minds: what is the point of what we are doing here at home? What kind of lasting impact will this really have?

Sometimes it becomes overwhelming as we feel the lack of appreciation and total lack of glamor. It all builds up and eventually leads to the inevitable conclusion that this must be all there really is in life. *Is* this all there is for my life—changing one hundred diapers a day, cleaning up trails of destruction, attempting to lose the baby weight, and somehow trying to find meaning and purpose in it all?

For me, it was hard to put a smile on my face when at church I was hearing about how the world is getting worse and worse. The news is the same way. You might notice that even Hollywood has jumped on the end-times bandwagon. The next time you take a trip to your local video rental store, check out how many flicks are about the end of the world. You will be astonished.

How exactly are we supposed to get through the day happy and chipper, singing "This is the day that the Lord has made," when all we know is that life on planet Earth is only going to get worse? *Is* the world really getting worse? If it's true the world is going to hell in a hand basket, there's really no point in trying very hard, is there?

Mixed Messages

Someone once coined the phrase, "You don't polish brass on a sinking ship." That implies two things: the world is nothing but a sinking ship, and there is no point in trying to make it any better. I heard that message all my life. If you're like me, you may have asked yourself these questions: Why work hard? It will all be lost. Why start a business? Why build churches? People will only tear them down. Why build up wealth as an inheritance for my kids one day? Satan owns all the money anyway. Besides, after the Rapture, it won't matter since we will be gone.

Oh, yeah—and why should we even bother to have children? We would only be bringing more victims of the Antichrist into the world. If there is some chance that the Rapture does not happen when they say it will, imagine—our children will have to endure the Great Tribulation! That used to be a big fear of mine. Eventually all these big questions led me to the mundane parts of my life: Why do dishes? Why make my bed? Why do anything? It is all for nothing in the end. Victory is nothing but a dream on this side of heaven. I might as well try to enjoy whatever I can while there is still time.

This was the mentality I had for years. I accepted defeat before I even got out of bed. I was spiritually depressed and oppressed with this type of thinking. Then I started noticing another Christian book trend. More and more books keep coming out with messages about positive thinking: "Think positive and good things will happen to you." It seems every month there is a new best-seller about how you can have your best life now, or how you can think and believe your way to success and a prosperous life. Hundreds of titles talk of God's will for everyone to be effortlessly healthy and wealthy and that "God has a wonderful plan for your life!" Just take a stroll through your local Christian bookstore and see all the works that include descriptions of overcoming challenges, moving forward, and having "victory" in life. Is it just me, or do these two prevalent messages seem schizophrenic? "The world is getting worse; the Antichrist is coming," and "God wants victory in your life! Just think positive!" Well, I wanted to know: which is it? They are completely opposing ideas.

I noticed the church teaches us to tell the world about Jesus, but when it comes to End Times, we warn the world that Jesus will lose the battle on Earth, at least until the very end. We teach them about the Great Commission, but also teach them the nations will never *actually* be discipled.

Maybe we don't say those exact words, but we certainly imply them through the theology we teach. Apparently, God planned to liberate only our souls and spirits with no intention of liberating the rest of His creation—or redeeming any of world history, for that matter.

We are instructed to tell new converts that one day Jesus will rule and reign, but He is not really sitting on the throne... technically... sort of... right now. Right now, Satan is "the god of this world" and he currently runs the show.

It is amazing to me how God continues to save people despite this message. I can only imagine how confusing it must be as a new believer these days. Once you get in the door, you have another clash of ideas to wade through. When it comes to what preoccupies Christians, it seems to me there are two prevalent trends: those who overemphasize spiritual experience and those who overemphasize the intellect.

What is especially disturbing to me as I look at these two prevailing trends is that, in both cases, Christians continue to *think* like *pagans*. We have believers walking out of healing centers and revival meetings, and believers walking out of Bible classes and seminary who *both* will go ahead and vote for an anti-Christian president. Both sides still make educational choices for their children that reflect the thinking of the world instead of the thinking of Christ. Millions of well-meaning, Jesus-loving people are Christian in their hearts, but heathen in their minds.

And it is not just in revival tents and seminaries that we see this disconnect, but also all across the board, Christians look just like the rest of the world. Sure, maybe we cleaned up our foul language and added some "Christianese" to our vocabulary. We may have the appearance of living a good, clean, moral life too. At the end of the day, however, we are no more Christ-like than the unbelievers we pray for, because we do not know how to *think* like Christians. We still think, decide, and choose the way the rest of the world does.

You see, the views we hold change everything. We want to be "sold out" for Jesus, but we have forgotten that we are to love the Lord in four ways: heart, soul, strength, and *mind*. We often forget that fourth component. Loving the Lord with our mind is not just thinking positively, and it is not about filling our heads with facts. What it really means is that every piece of data that comes into our brains, whether mathematical or moral, whether it is the news, media, books, paintings we see, or even those crossword puzzles we solve—all information that enters our brain we are to compare and analyze through the mind of Christ. That is the definition of loving the Lord our God with our mind. This means that there is no such thing as neutral information.

The myth of neutrality will be a recurring theme in this book. If we believe the God of the universe created all things, then His stamp is on every little fact of life. It means the alphabet points to Christ. It means the laws of nature point to Christ. It means the bacteria in our intestines point to Christ. There is nothing in life that is neutral because the Creator is not neutral. He is "I Am" and He wants *all of us*—not just our emotions, not just our intellect. He wants our entire beings.

If we look in Christian bookstores, it is easy to see the clash of ideas within Christendom. I call it the battle-of-the-book-shelves: There is the "end is near" shelf and the "create your own reality" shelf. One line of thought cuts off the promise of God's victory for the future, and the other attempts to play God and create its own victory—to create its own version of the future by speaking things into existence. What I wanted to know was what does God really have in store for me? What is God's purpose for all Christian moms in this place in time? Why has He placed us here and now? What has He actually promised for our day and age? If the end is near, why bother? On the other hand, if I can simply create my own reality, why do I need Christ? If I am not effortlessly successful, rich and wise, is it because I did not have enough faith?

Jigsaw Puzzle Faith

I needed answers. I needed real purpose. I needed vision for the future. There was once a very dark time in my life. I was living in a spiritual prison, wrapped in chains. These chains held me down and choked the life out of me. I could not function like that anymore, but I did not think there was a way out.

I had no idea I had allowed myself to be taken captive in the first place. I had no clue that God was going to cut me from my bonds and put these specific questions in my brain so that I would have no choice but to seek out the right answers. I had no idea these answers would affect my husband, my children, my friends, and all our future descendants. The answers to these questions would ring through generations. The answers would change the course of history, not just in our little corner of the world, but, like an earthquake in the deep ocean, would create waves that travel for a long while, and eventually create a tsunami that leaves a lasting impact forever.

If you are a homemaker, a mom, or someone who is looking for a deeper meaning and purpose in life—if you seek to understand your place in history and your significance in the big picture—then this book is for you. My life completely turned upside down when I finally saw the big picture. For

Doom, Gloom, a Mop & a Broom

many of us, it is as though we dumped out a five-thousand-piece puzzle on the table and lost the box it came in. How successful are we going to be at putting it together without the picture on the box? Not very. We need the big picture in order to see how the pieces fit. It is the only way. Solving the puzzle is a big task. Even choosing to look at the big picture is not easy. It involves examining the theology we hold. It involves breaking strongholds that stifle us and hold us back from our true purpose because of our lack of knowledge. It involves leveling myths and exposing lies we have heard all our lives about "The End Times."

In my own puzzle piece journey, I learned about many things I never thought I would care to know. I learned what a Christian worldview is, what it means to defend the faith, how important it is to understand "humanism," and how God wants me to disciple my children. I even discovered what God thinks about education, politics, music, pizza delivery and God's plan for the future of the church on Earth. You know—just average housewife stuff.

While these issues *may not be* the average homemaker topic of the day, I believe it soon will be. Satan tries to keep housewives from learning this stuff. When we don't care about these things, he wins a big battle. The devil is thrilled when he observes us Christian women wrapped up in the drama of our own lives, or when the highlight of our week is catching the latest episode of our favorite show, or when we don't know what is going on in the world. To him, it means we forfeit the real game. We retreat. I found out that this is not God's plan. He has something much bigger in store for us!

Do you want to know how you—a wife and mom—can change the whole world? Are you tired of meaningless Facebook and blogging drama? Do you want to know what you can do differently today that will affect the whole culture around you? Do you want to know why the end is *not* near and how there is an amazing and bright future for us?

If you do, hang on tight. Get ready for a challenge. We are going to delve into some deep topics. We are going to look at what it is we really believe: our theology. It might be a brain workout for you. Maybe it won't be. You might not like what you hear. Maybe after a few chapters you close this book and resolve never to read another page. That would be easy to do. There was a time when I might have done that myself.

Nevertheless, if you want to be a history-making mom, if you want change in your life, if you want real meaning, significance, and fulfillment in the short time you have on earth, I challenge you to finish this book.

There are some very important ideas here that could change everything. They are God's ideas. Many Bible scholars have written huge volumes on these topics. I have condensed some of these big ideas into one small book and put them into what I hope are bite-size portions for us busy moms.

I pray what I am about to share with you will enrich your life, enlighten your mind, excite your heart, and help you gain new insight into your destiny as a world-changer. Changing the world is not just your destiny; it is your duty!

CHAPTER 2

Spirals & Ghosts

The beginning of my journey to a victorious future found me at rock bottom. It may have been a slow spiral to that point, but it seems I was there for a long portion of my life. I grew up in a typical Christian home in an area we call the "Bible belt" of southern British Columbia, Canada. For many years, I went to a non-denominational church and private Christian school. My parents divorced by the time I was 11 or so, and this was the beginning of my descent.

I spent my 'tween years totally boy-crazy. I remember wanting to date at the age of twelve. Looking back, I wonder how my parents didn't see that coming. I was lonely, hurting, ripped from a real family and was looking for an escape. By the time I was 15, I was at a crossroad in my life. I did love the Lord; I wanted to serve Him. Unfortunately, there had been much church and family drama. Though I originally had strong roots, I was losing my way.

My parents were preoccupied with their own disorientation from a failed marriage and church politics in the mix of it. They were losing my heart and did not see it happening. Eventually, temptations came at me and I was not equipped to handle them. In the maze of being lost and strongheaded, I was certain of my independence. I was certain I wanted to be an adult. I was certain I wanted to enjoy all the "freedoms" that adults enjoyed. I gradually rebelled.

It was a slow process, but it happened. It wasn't hard for me to get access to drugs and alcohol, though I was mostly too afraid to dabble with drugs. I found out very quickly how a young woman can use her looks and demeanor to get things. I thought it empowered me, but it only doomed me.

Among many scenarios that were very dangerous and damaging to me, I also ended up 16 and pregnant. I was completely ashamed. However, I wanted to be an adult, so even that made me feel grown up in a way.

My boyfriend at the time had backslidden in his faith, and this event caused him to return to the Lord. He was ready to take responsibility and submit to his church. That was a rare thing.

After the news had spread and everyone in the family and church found out, I miscarried at around sixteen weeks. I had a feeling something was wrong a week or two previously. I saw the doctors, but they assured me everything was fine. The miscarriage was traumatic for me. I had to sit in the ER waiting room, hemorrhaging and laboring for approximately six hours before a doctor could see me (the reality of Canadian socialized health care). I received no pain relief. That experience was totally traumatizing to me as a sixteen-year-old.

While recovering, about a week later, I had my first anxiety attack. I thought I was dying. I could hardly breathe and my limbs and face were numb. My heart was skipping beats and this "black" feeling came upon me. I went to the hospital. They gave me something to relax me. It worked. I felt normal again. They confirmed it was only a panic attack, but that now I was anemic, having lost a lot of blood from the miscarriage. I nearly needed a transfusion. That panic attack was the first of many to come. The doctor prescribed me a take-as-needed medication for my panic attacks. The problem was that I was having them every day, sometimes several times a day. So I took the medication a lot. Before long, I was completely dependent on it. I was also grieving and looking for an escape and used the medication in excess.

Somewhere around that time, the doctors put me on anti-depressants as well. That turned me into a complete space cadet. I behaved strangely, and said and did things I am embarrassed about now (though I do not recall many specifics). My parents were worried I might harm myself and had me put into the hospital, where the doctors cut me off my medication, except for the anti-depressants. It didn't help much, but they were able to see that I was not going to harm myself, so after about a week I went home.

After that, I went to stay with a Christian family to get away from negative influences. Initially it was good for me, but I ruined the experience when I decided I would rather be with my boyfriend. He picked me up and we went back home. I did not stop partying for some time, although my thoughts were a little clearer than before. I was mostly in so much emotional pain I did not know how to handle it. Eventually I ended the relationship on my own.

Next, I entered a two-year on-and-off relationship with an ex-Jehovah's Witness turned atheist. I knew the whole time I should not be with him, but there was a strong attraction and he was so unpredictable, irrational, and shocking that I believe I became addicted to the adrenaline of the relationship itself. An adrenaline-junkie with a panic-attack problem: not a good combination. I lost a lot of weight. When I finally realized that our religious differences would never work out in the end, I saw that I needed to clean up my life and repent. I knew I had to return to God. I had put it off for a long while because I liked my current drug of choice (the bad boyfriend).

I eventually moved back home. I also decided I needed to finish my GED. I got a job. I went back to church. I got some counseling. I filled journals with all my emotions. I was still very lost, but I was on my way. I was beginning to heal a little. Reading the Bible was like a first-aid kit for my soul. I felt so tainted by the world. To this day, I still have to remind myself that Jesus died for all my sins and washed me clean as pure snow.

ROAD TO REDEMPTION

I believe with all my heart that my complete restoration and redemption took place on my wedding day. I met my husband very suddenly. I was enjoying a new set of Christian friends. Friends who didn't party and enjoyed things like playing live music and going to Bible studies. One day my friends invited me out to a local hockey game. One guy mentioned that his cousin had just moved to our town that day and would be joining us. I didn't think much of it at all.

I met Steve in the parking lot. It was definitely one of those moments where I knew in my spirit that there would be something significant between us. We were always in a group for the first while, and I wish it had continued longer, as I have the best memories from that time. It wasn't long before Steve and I knew we wanted to get married.

He proposed to me Christmas Eve in 2004 and we were married in April of 2005. I felt like I had gone through hell and back, but on my wedding day I felt like a queen for the first time in my life. I felt like I was finally restored to the Leah God had made. I no longer felt tainted and ashamed. I stood before God and two hundred people, publicly redeemed by joining my husband in marriage. It truly was one of the happiest days of my life.

This may be coincidence, but my panic attacks left me at that time. To this day, I do not know or understand what caused them, but since getting married, I have not had a problem. While I have certainly experienced anxiety, it has never again escalated into a scary attack. It is as if God gave me roots and sank them into the ground by making me whole through my husband.

Within three months of marriage, we had started a carpentry business and found out we were expecting. We were very excited. I was nine months pregnant on our first anniversary. We were so happy to become a family of three.

God took the broken and ashamed girl, healed her wounds, put a beautiful dress on her and placed a crown on her head. I entered motherhood with my whole heart. It was hard at times adjusting to being a wife and mother. I had never seen or experienced what a healthy marriage should be like. I had to learn about the responsibilities all at once, without any experience or many examples around.

Beyond the pain of growing and adapting and nurturing a new marriage, we still had to deal with the worldly baggage that we both brought into the marriage. God is faithful to redeem, but sometimes there are still consequences for our actions. At times, I had trouble emotionally letting go of my past. Old feelings would come up occasionally and I did not know how to deal with them. My husband was so gracious to me and forgave me. God knew I needed a man with a tender heart. Since then, God has been faithful to continue healing both of us from our pasts.

THE GHOST OF BAD-THEOLOGY PAST

Our son had just turned one when we found out we were expecting again. We were hoping for a sister for him and that's exactly what we got. (I prayed a little prayer.) During my pregnancy with our second child, some theological ghosts came back to haunt me. From the time I was a pre-teen, I had a fear of "End Times." Initially, the book of Revelation fascinated me, but that fascination turned to fear and depression when I heard horror stories about a future "Antichrist" and a "Great Tribulation."

The book series *Left Behind* by Tim LaHaye had come out and seemed to be everywhere. Even though it was popular, I heard somewhere that not everyone believed the *Left Behind* view of end times was biblical. I was very confused, but too afraid to study it.

Of course, it didn't help when in youth group and Bible class we dreamed up imaginary torture scenarios of Christians persecuted for not receiving the "mark of the beast." It didn't help when we watched videos like *Thief in the Night* either. Bad theology and a wild imagination make a dangerous combination. I felt traumatized and afraid of what terrible things might happen in my lifetime.

In fact, I believe this great fear was part of what led me down my path of rebellion. In part, my thinking was this: "Well, if the world is going to hell in a hand basket and there's nothing I can do about it, I might as well enjoy whatever I can right now." My entire teen years might have looked completely different had someone taught me what the Bible really says about the matter.

So much had this childhood fear affected me that, back in 2006, when we brought our first baby home from the hospital, I felt bad for this baby.

I had an awful feeling of guilt for bringing an innocent baby into a world where he would have to endure the Antichrist. The thought actually crossed my mind that we had been selfish and irresponsible for having a baby!

I had to move on the best I could, so I would ignore my fear of the end times for as long as I could distract myself. Then I would hear something on the radio, or I would see something in a movie. If it happened to be related in any way, shape, or form to the future, perhaps something cataclysmic or apocalyptic, it would trigger my end-times-madness phobia. I would get a surge of adrenaline and literally want to hide under a blanket. Sometimes it made me mad that I was still having end-times nightmares as a grown adult. I would still wake in the night in tears and need prayer because I was so afraid of what was going to happen.

Life almost didn't feel worth living. I was terrified of bar codes because someone told me those were the alleged "mark of the beast." Everywhere I looked, there were bar codes. So of course I thought I was going insane. I felt so alone. It seemed as though no one experienced the fears I was experiencing. No one had any good answers either. The usual reply of "God is in control" did not console me at all. I had typed out every fear-related scripture in the Bible and posted them everywhere. I still couldn't escape it.

I went to counseling and they tried to appease my fear by convincing me to believe in the Rapture. They gave me the best evidence they could muster up for it. I went home and began to dig a little. All through my second pregnancy, I was searching for truth. I had always been afraid to search this out, but was even more determined not to bring another baby into the world with the feeling of guilt, sadness, and defeat. I needed answers.

THE BEGINNING OF THE END

One time, I awoke in the night after I had a bad dream about being chased down by men who wanted to kill me for not receiving the "mark" and I was asking the Lord the same question I had asked for years: "Why, Lord? Why have You put me through this? Why are You letting me suffer with this fear? Why do You torture me? I want the truth, Lord Jesus. I don't care what it is, I just want the truth!" This is the only time I can remember when I received an immediate answer to one of my prayers. In that moment, two Scriptures were impressed upon my mind: *Then you will know the truth, and the truth will set you free* (John 8:32); and *God has not given us a spirit of fear, but of power and of love and of a sound mind* (2 Tim. 1:7).

I had read those scriptures dozens of times before; however, this time I felt the Lord gave me a specific insight about them. This is what first came to mind: "The Bible says that when I know the truth, it will set me free. Am I free? Absolutely not! I can safely conclude that I have yet to find the truth. I am not free about this matter because I do not know the truth about it." Well, that settled that. This was the insight for the second scripture: "When I do know the truth and have been set free, this is the fruit that I will bear: power, love, and a sound mind." I understood this to mean a couple things:

1. I will be empowered where fear has robbed me.

His divine power has given to us all things that pertain to life and godliness, through the knowledge of Him . . . (2 Pet. 1:3).

2. When fear no longer robs me, I will finally be able to pursue my calling and my ministry: my family. I will be empowered to do all things pertaining to life and godliness through the knowledge of Him. Love would replace my fear.

There is no fear in love; but perfect love casts out fear, because fear involves torment. But he who fears has not been made perfect in love (1 John 4:18). Until my fear was gone, I would not be able to understand God's love for me, or be able to love my family in the way I knew God wanted.

3. When I understood the truth about this matter, I would receive a sound mind. Some translations say *self-control*. Either way, I took this to mean that when I understood the truth, my emotions would not be the driving force of my will. This turned out to be very true. To this day, I still have little triggers that go off occasionally, but the difference is that now, when my inner emotions do a little roller coaster, my mind says, "No. Look at what the Bible really says. Look at the future God has promised you and your descendants. Now look at the victory He has given you. Go and accomplish this." My emotional response quickly dissipates. Good theology saved me from insanity. I now have a greater measure of self-control over irrational emotions.

But also for this very reason, giving all diligence, add to your faith virtue, to virtue knowledge, to knowledge self-control, to self-control perseverance, to perseverance godliness, to godliness brotherly kindness, and to brotherly kindness love (2 Pet. 1:5–9).

This scripture shows the relationship between godly knowledge affecting self-control. That is exactly what happened to me. Once I understood what the truth was, and what God really had in store for me, my family, and all of our descendants, I finally experienced freedom. I then experienced the fruit of that freedom: power, love, and a sound mind. Hallelujah!

Archeological Truth-Digging

After I received this understanding of what God wanted to do for me, I was ready to dig for truth. I was ready to leave depression behind me. I was ready to kick fear out the door and embrace what God had for me. I was ready to engage in my purpose. It began when I opened the door of eschatology (which means the study of future things or "End Times") and then ten more doors opened. It was time to break out the shovel and excavation gear.

The journey ahead of me was harder than I expected, but more rewarding than I could ever have imagined. I was on a quest for truth, a quest for meaning, real purpose in life, and a legacy. I had no idea where God was leading me, or why He allowed all my experiences. I have only begun to see it now. What I do know is that the long-term effects of what He has taught me are going to be staggering. It will affect my children and many generations down the line. I am on a mission now. The quest is clear. It is true, the road is narrow, but it is also well defined. Now I know where we're going and I know how we're going to get there. We are at war. The outcome has already been determined. We need only to obey. Victory is ours.

CHAPTER 3

Dominoes of Destiny

So there I was—a new wife and mother. Though God had healed me in many ways, my spiritual life was still limping. I wanted to be full of joy, but I was not sure how to feel about the present or the future. For many years, I thought the end of the world was just around the corner. I believed things were getting worse in the world and didn't know what to do with myself.

As I explained in the last chapter, it was hard not to think about it constantly, since every time I looked at a newspaper, heard a preacher, or turned on the TV, it seemed like the end was coming any time. Every day it was a nagging thought that wouldn't leave me alone. I often felt defeated before I even got out of bed.

Soon, other worldly thinking started to enter my mind. I was a young, stay-at-home-mom and remember people frequently asking me, "So… when do you plan on going back to work?" I remember the look of shock when I told them I had no plans of returning to "work" if I could help it.

Why were people surprised by this? I started to feel a subtle pressure both in Christian and non-Christian circles, and it confused me. I thought Christians would understand that the family is the backbone of society. When the family unit is unhealthy, dysfunctional or even destroyed, the rest of civilization inevitably falls apart.

Though I believed in being a stay-at-home-mom in theory, even with little hope for the future, I succumbed to thoughts of what life would be like had I not gotten married and had children. Other women my age were out having a great time, travelling the world, pursuing their whims and desires, getting university degrees and living the good life. These women were "free," unlike me. They weren't stuck at home, looking frumpy, changing diapers, cleaning up messes all day, and being the occasional landing place of vomit.

I started thinking about all the things I wished I could be doing but couldn't because of my husband and children. I had always wanted to travel and now I would not have the chance for who knows how many years. I always wanted to go to university. I especially wanted to pursue my music career. I'd been a songwriter and singer since the age of thirteen, but now, because of my new life obligations, I would never be able to pursue my dreams. I succumbed to the temptation of depression and resentment.

In addition, I felt guilty because many women I knew seemed like they were born to be mothers and wives. Being a wife and mother was their ultimate life's goal and mission. They were what I called "naturals," feeling this role brought them complete satisfaction and fulfillment. I was a failure compared to these women. Being a wife and mother did not come naturally to me at all. While I was certainly born with maternal instincts, I had a drive and passion to do something "bigger" than myself. Somehow raising a family wasn't big enough. It was just ordinary.

If the only thing I ever accomplished in my life was being a wife and a mom—even if I raised a great family—no one would remember my name in a hundred years. No one would ever know who I was in the world, except in my own little circle. At the end of my life, there would be no award ceremony, no public acknowledgements, no raises or promotions to look back on. Just a simple little gravestone. I hated the thought that the world would not know my name.

When a Bad Day Becomes a Lifestyle

Day after day, I gave in to this way of thinking. It became easy for me to find flaws in my husband and I grew to resent him. I also began to resent being stuck at home with my children. As this grew in my heart, other terrible thoughts came to me: thoughts about what would happen if I just left and started a new life. I immediately repented for it even entering my head. I tried not to entertain these thoughts, but I fought them from time to time. The days seemed never-ending and I longed for something more. The future seemed grim. "The end of the world is probably around the corner," I thought. "Great! I'm stuck at home as a maid and a cook with no future."

I don't believe in blaming everything on Satan, and think we often give him too much credit—but I believe that sometimes thoughts are hurled at us that are not our own. To this day, when I am especially struggling, I am more susceptible to entertaining bad thoughts. The fact that terrible thoughts sometimes enter our brains does not mean we have sinned. What matters is what we do with those thoughts. Do we make them captive to Christ—or do we sink into self-pity and entertain the thoughts?

Some days, I dwell on bitter thoughts, but I immediately recognize it, so I repent and make them captive to Christ. I take a breath of fresh air, make a cup of tea, then hug my kids and pray with them. Then I move on. Some days it is not that easy. Some days every second is a struggle. I recently told my husband that raising four kids under the age of six is by far the hardest thing I have ever done in my whole life. I had no idea what it would entail. I still feel totally unprepared, unqualified, and inadequate.

Once in a blue moon, I feel like Super Mom. Usually it is only because I managed to get myself dressed, everyone fed (without any major squabbles), *and* I accomplished a few chores. Often, I am again humbled the next day.

This is just everyday life for any stay-at-home mom. From a practical standpoint, life is easier than it has ever been with all our modern-day conveniences, yet somehow discontentment overflows in our society. We must ask ourselves this question: what happens when a bad day becomes a habit?

If we are struggling with our attitude and perpetually giving in to negativity, it creates a pattern. It is like a vacuum vortex that sucks us in and whirls us around, down the deep spiral of inner dissatisfaction. It spews out an atmosphere in the home. It creates a hostile mood within the marriage. It makes our children's mother a monster. This is not a battle that a woman faces only a few times in her life; for many, it is every day. It is a battle we must *win* every day. What if, years from now, we could look back and see how this simple daily decision affected our great-grandchildren for the better or worse?

I'd always been taught Biblical truths regarding the family, but in reality, I just didn't feel it. I knew it was right, but it seemed difficult and almost pointless to put into practice. So I began to systematically revisit many of those teachings and tried to look at them with new eyes. I asked God to renew my tired mind and help me see what I was missing.

THE RIPPLE EFFECT

The healthy family is the backbone of all society—I understood that. Starting with individuals, the family is the foundation for a healthy church, a happy community and a well-functioning government. Just like a row of dominoes, when we see a breakdown in government and society at one end, we know right away that it is a long-term result of the breakdown of the family at the other end. Since marriage is the institution set up by God, when marriages break down, it contributes to societal corruption and decay on a grand scale.

For example, divorce tears a family apart spiritually and physically. The children are forever fragmented. Because of the pain and damage, many children grow up to reject the institution of marriage, and thus we see the rise of cohabitation and the decrease of actual marriages taking place. Some of these children grow to altogether reject God and His principles for how we ought to live our lives. All these contributing factors affect the way these broken individuals think about life, the way they view the world, and even the way they vote.

If broken people get married or even just live together and have children, they pass along their broken belief system about God and the world. If those people divorce as well (which statistics show is likely), a double fragment passes down. Now we have a second generation of broken worldviews and broken homes. If the children of those homes perpetuate the cycle, we now have a third generation of people with a tainted and skewed worldview, and the damage to society grows exponentially. This is literally happening today. Some of you know this to be all too true. These dozens and hundreds and then thousands of people make up the communities which make up our society and our civilization.

If you think about it, so much is at stake when a marriage goes bad. Broken children eventually grow up. They might become scientists. If they have rejected God, they might pursue a career that rejects God in His creation and teach more children to do the same. Perhaps those broken kids grow up to become broken lawyers. If they have rejected God and His standards, they may make a career out of trying to legalize immorality and outlaw righteousness. Those broken people may become business owners, retail operators, or construction workers, and if they have a skewed view of God and the world, they may choose lifestyles that are hostile to God. They may reject children by aborting them, vote in a way that would bring destruction to others, and likely perpetuate atheism.

In general, broken people make broken choices. It all goes back to the family. The family starts with the God-sanctioned institute of marriage as He defines it. You can see how society really hangs on marriage. It was the first institution God created. It is why God gave the death penalty for adultery and homosexuality. Those acts are direct attempts at destroying a whole civilization because they destroy marriage and the family.

Why You Need to Know About Secular Humanism

If you pay attention, you might notice there is a war against biblical marriage. We keep seeing the courts trying to redefine words, especially when it comes to family. We saw this when the word "baby" became "fetus." When you use this definition, it is easier to make people believe a baby is not a real, living soul, but only a clump of cells.

This is the same reason people are trying so hard to change the meaning of the word "marriage." Since marriage is a biblical concept and the method through which God builds societies, people who reject God need to separate the word from its religious source. They need to replace it with their own "modern" definition so they don't have to be accountable to anyone. They want to do their own thing.

The courts also keep trying to change the meaning of other family definitions like "mother," "father," "boy" and "girl." We are seeing this take place more and more in schools across America.

In reality, this type of maneuver seeks to destroy God's pre-ordained order. When we pass laws saying every public school child will learn that gay, lesbian, and transgender lifestyles are "normal" and appropriate ways of defining "family," this is the work of something evil. The issue is not "human rights"…it is more insidious than that. In a general sense, the Bible calls it rebellion against God. More specifically, it is a philosophy called "Secular Humanism." I will be referring to this term a lot in this book.

Secular Humanism (we will just call it humanism for short) is *the belief that man is god*. If this term is new to you, think of it as a religious cult or belief system—just like Mormonism, atheism, or New Age religion. People live by this philosophy, sometimes without being aware of it.

Of course, there are those who definitely know and understand what they believe. That is why we call it a religion, even though most humanists don't like calling it a religion. Humanism rejects all religion and insists that morality, thought, and reason can exist outside of God. It is similar to atheism, but a little different in that atheism is simply the denial of belief in God. Humanism denies the existence of God and addresses all of life with a specific philosophy. Atheism then, is just what humanists believe concerning God, but humanism has a lot more to say than just that. Humanism is one of the fastest growing ideologies in our society. This is why it is especially dangerous and sneaky: it is not always a formal belief in someone's head. Many people are humanists without knowing it.

There are even humanists within the church. The self-aware humanist recognizes one of their chief objectives is to rid every ounce of religion from the world, especially in government. They really believe that all forms of religion are bad for the world, that it hurts people and that the world would be a better place without it.

There are many ways humanists will try to achieve this, and one way includes the redefinition of words. When language is redefined, there is a change in the way society thinks about things. If, over a period of fifty to one hundred years, we all shift our thinking about the word "marriage" from meaning "a covenant between God, man and woman," to meaning, "two people who sign a paper and get tax benefits," a revolution has taken place. It is a very subtle and very powerful way of changing a society without anyone really noticing or opposing it.

Some humanists may not even be aware that this is what they believe. Maybe they just think that everything should be "neutral" and leave religion out of it. Either way, they believe that man is the ultimate determiner of truth. Humanism places man equal with God. It places man *as* God.

Every cult and religious philosophy has a beginning. They all originated at the Fall when Adam and Eve sinned, but they manifest in different ways throughout the course of history. When we hear about a new cult or religion, it's not really *new*. Humanism is as old as time; it's the exact scenario Satan presented Adam and Eve when he told them they could be like God.

The fathers of humanism understood that if they could break down the biblical family unit, they could destroy God's society. If they destroyed God's society, they could set up man's society. This has happened numerous times in history, and has never gone over well with God! It is very possible to achieve this end with no war. If you can teach people to think in a different way, you have won a war, albeit silently. It only takes time to set in. Humanists go about this through language. They want to change the meaning of words so they really have no meaning at all. When words and ideas have no meaning, they have no purpose. When life and things have no purpose, and people become hopeless, it is much easier to gain control.

In the end, Secular Humanists lust after the oldest thing in the world: corrupt power. This is nothing new—it is as old as history. People continue to reject God and His standard by trying to re-mould society. They want to change it so they can escape accountability to their Creator. However, if you observe history, you will see examples of societies that succeeded in their agenda for a time, but God faithfully brought destruction and ruin upon them.

The problem—and the issue I really want to address—is when Christians are part of the corruption. When Christians sit on the sidelines, allowing evil to flourish, when they believe God will "rapture" them out of the mess, when they just sit back and relax, or when they blatantly partake in the disobedience and the forsaking of God's standards, God does not spare them from His punishment. His judgment will not fall on both the godly and the ungodly, but why should He spare His people if they have become rebels? If they have participated in the undoing of a nation, and if they have made the same lifestyle choices as His enemies, why should God spare them? Why should God rescue us from persecution when our own inactivity and apathy in the world brought it upon us in the first place? Should God rescue people who say they love Him but are really humanists?

Matthew 5:13 says, "You are the salt of the earth. But if the salt loses its saltiness, how can it be made salty again? It is no longer good for anything, except to be thrown out and trampled by men."

Salt is a preservative. It gives food shelf life. Preservation is synonymous with the biblical concept of dominion and stewardship. If Christians fail to preserve the earth by upholding God's commands, and if we fail to take dominion of the earth as God would have us do it, the Bible says we are good for nothing except to be thrown out and trampled by men. That is quite a rebuke for those of us who prefer to sit on the sidelines.

If this humanism stuff sounds scary to you—good! As moms and wives, we need to see the real and present dangers in this world so we can protect our families and plan for the future. If we want to change the world, we have to take a deep breath, brace ourselves, and be aware of the devil's schemes so we can resist him! It is about being prepared. This is part of our spiritual warfare. If we do not have our guard up, or if this kind of thing surprises us, it means our heads are in the sand. We need to look to the horizon and see the big picture of what God is doing and what Satan is doing. If we know how Satan is going to try to ensnare us, we can anticipate his attack. All the surprise is gone and he has no power.

I think Satan's biggest weapon *is* surprise. If he can keep moms and wives from seeing or caring about things like humanism, he can jump out of the bushes one day and surprise-attack us like a ninja. However, he does not have any real weapon except keeping Christians ignorant. He just looks scary and jumps out of bushes yelling, "Hey!" So, if we want to really get ahead of the devil and his surprise attacks, we need to see what he's trying to do with marriages and families.

If the destruction of a nation starts with the destruction of our marriages and families, then the rebuilding of a nation begins with the rebuilding of our marriages and families. As wives, we must do our part, and it all starts with asking God to help us change our attitudes. If we are bitter, resentful, and angry about our lives, it will undermine the marriage. If we submit to God's authority in our lives; accept the places we are given; and choose joy, contentment, and pleasure in serving, we will contribute to the building of a whole society. It seems so small and insignificant. It is easy to ask why one person or family matters in the grand scheme of things. I hope to show you how much your single family truly does make a difference.

There came a time when I had to make a decision. Maybe you are at this point now. I had to decide if I would remain miserably attached to my family. I had to decide if I would entertain evil thoughts which would lead to devastating choices, or choose to embrace the life I had been given.

I considered the consequences. I saw that if I emotionally rejected and resented my family, the price to pay would not be just mine, but the generations to come. If I embraced my role, I could very well become the female cornerstone of a future godly society.

Either way, and every day, my choices would have a ripple effect.

CHAPTER 4

How To Be a Queen

Are you tired of living in a screwed up world? Pay attention to this chapter. Much power lies within your own hands. God has chosen you. You are perhaps a wife and a mother (or a future wife and mother if you are single). Even women who are unable to have children have maternal instincts and have used them for the glory of God, spiritually adopting people and leaving lasting impressions. Look how many people Mother Theresa affected!

Women are born to love and serve. They are born to nurture. They are born to have that tender touch that magically fixes everything. Women are born to be slaves in the kitchen. Just kidding! I had to make sure you were still paying attention. Women are not slaves in their homes *ever*, but instead, they pride themselves with womanly tasks of "domestic engineering." They make things work and run smoothly. They put their feminine touch on the walls, the bedrooms, the tables, and everywhere you can see. They make a house a home. They make their man feel like a real king. They love to do this because it is the most fulfilling job they can do.

Okay, maybe some of this is what we strive for, but it is definitely our calling. Some of us really struggle with that calling. Some of us get the itch every now and then to "break free" and just get away from our husband and kids. I know I have felt that way from time to time. I have also noticed it very easily turns into a habit of negative thinking where you feel the need for this "freedom" all the time. This can lead many places, and some of them are dangerous. I have come to the realization that, often, the very thing I have wanted a "break" from is the very thing that brings me sanity and stability in life.

If it weren't for my husband and kids, for whom I must "slave in the kitchen," I would likely fray at both ends and who knows where I would be right now. Having a family forces me to be responsible. It forces me to mature and grow. It forces me to take a serious look at the implications of my life—or lack of them. Having these "obligations" has kept me from becoming possibly the most selfish person on the planet. That is why we have to consider the gravity of our biblical role in our home. It is our true calling.

Have you ever considered how wives and mothers are, in a sense, the cornerstone of our whole civilization? Have you ever thought about how a woman's role contributes to the advancement or breakdown of an entire society? It is true.

Before we talk about how awesome women are, I would like to acknowledge the critical role of husbands and fathers. There is an attack on all things masculine. There is an agenda to turn our boys into girly wimps. We saw in the previous chapter that humanists want to redefine words like "masculine" and "feminine" so they have no meaning. This is the opposite of what God wants. Instead of making everything "gender neutral," we need a great awakening of boys who will become real men. We need boys who know how to lead at young ages, as in former generations, in case something happens to dad or while he is away.

There are many stories in the last century of boys no older than twelve who had to take upon themselves the task of providing for their families, leading and keeping them safe. They had guns and they knew how to use them. They had skills and understood basic commerce and business. They were young entrepreneurs.

Yes, desperate times may have placed those boys in such a position, but compare the ability and skills of those boys to the twelve-year-olds we have now. Some twelve-year-olds today hardly know how to make their own beds. They still get "time outs." They are babies in mentality and have virtually no responsibilities.

The world system has taught that it is cruel and unusual for kids to have any responsibility. "Experts" tell us kids should enjoy childhood, free of any worries since adulthood will come soon enough. There is a serious long-term problem with that advice. It will produce incompetent adults. It then takes those adults twice as long to learn the hard lessons of life, thus delaying the good they might accomplish for God's Kingdom. Incompetent adults often delay marriage because of immaturity, making them even less appealing as possible mates. No one wants to marry a man with the maturity of a fourteen-year-old, or a grown man whose mother still does his laundry and has a permanent bachelor mentality.

When you think even more long-term, the delay of marriage results in the delaying of children too, which has exponential consequences when you consider the birth rates among competing religions hostile to Christianity. It is important that Christians have more children.

I think God put a natural instinct in us to desire marriage while we are young and to have kids right away. It is all a part of the dominion mandate God gave us (Gen. 1:28; 9:1–3). It's only our modern society that has influenced us to wait a long time to get married, and then wait even longer before we decide we're "ready" to have kids.

I want to say for the record that while this book is all about how homemakers can change the world, I believe that strong self-respecting women submit to and obey their husbands. That is where a huge revolution will begin. Do not mistake submission for being a doormat. That is unbiblical too. There are gazillions of books written on biblical womanhood and manhood, so I won't spend much time here. I will make the note though, that while both men and women are equal citizens in the Kingdom, we have different roles and responsibilities. When men return to leading women as they ought and take on the role of biblical head, God will bless our nation again. This is not *our* design, but *God's* design.

Men are born to lead. And yes, they have authority over us. The reason that idea makes us cringe is because of what happened at the Fall. It did not make Eve cringe *before* she sinned, but afterwards it did. God has always designed marriage to work this way, right from the beginning. It did not change later as the result of the curse. Our attitudes did, though. We are co-rulers with our husband, but we need to submit ourselves to his authority with joy.

Control Freaks

So while we consider how important it is that our men be real men and leaders of both home and society, let us consider how women influence those men. There is a *huge* difference between godly influence and worldly manipulation. Make sure to understand this distinction. If we understand our God-given ability to influence for the better, this will be a real key to understanding how women play a pivotal role in society.

We will start with Adam and Eve. Consider the eternal effects of Eve's deception and Adam's sin. If Adam was present at the time Eve ate the forbidden fruit (and the Genesis account implies this), he passively allowed her to fall to her spiritual death and failed in his responsibility to protect her.

Eve's failure is certain. In her offering the fruit to Adam, she tempted him—although she herself was deceived—to sin. And he chose to sin. As a result, they both brought down the entire human race in sin and death. That is the subtle power a woman can have. As part of the consequence for sinning, God said, "I will sharpen the pain of your pregnancy, and in pain you will give birth. And you will desire to control your husband, but he will rule over you" (Gen. 3:16; New Living Translation).

This was the beginning of the feminist movement. It is the heart of modern-day paganism—Mother Earth worship—and other cults centered on the "goddess" movement. That might sound weird, but when women elevate themselves and put themselves on a pedestal, and outside of the God-ordained sphere, it results in many weird ideas.

The fall of humankind was the beginning of a constant head-butting for control and authority. The woman now tries to exert her own authority, driven by the mentality that she does not need a man over her. "I can kill my own snakes," and "I can take care of myself" is the attitude many women have today, even within the church.

I really learned something when I read what Matthew Henry had to say about the change in Eve's attitude before and after the Fall. We all face the same struggle. Here is what he wrote about Genesis 3:16:

> [Eve] is here put into a state of subjection. The whole sex, which by creation was equal with man, is for sin, made inferior, and forbidden to usurp authority, 1 Tim. 2:11, 12. The wife particularly is hereby put under the dominion of her husband and is not *sui-juris*—at her own disposal . . . . This sentence amounts only to that command, "Wives, be in subjection to your husbands"; but the entrance of sin has made that duty a punishment, which otherwise it would not have been. *If man had not sinned, he would always have ruled with wisdom and love; and, if the woman had not sinned, she would always have obeyed with humility and meekness*; and then the dominion would have been no grievance, but our own sin and folly make our yoke heavy. If Eve had not eaten the forbidden fruit herself, and tempted her husband to eat it, she would never have complained of her subjection; therefore it ought never to be complained of, though harsh; but sin must be complained of, that made it so. Those wives who not only despise and disobey their husbands, but domineer over them, do not consider that they not only violate a divine law, but thwart a divine sentence.[1]

He points out that it is a sin to despise your husband or disobey him. When we domineer over him, we have gone a whole step further in our rebellion. We need to remember that rebellion is as serious a sin as witchcraft (1 Sam. 15:23). Yikes! I constantly have to remind myself about this. It is so easy to tell our husbands what to do or how to do it. It is so easy to complain when they don't do something "right." It is easy to be negative. Sometimes we need a wake-up call to remind us that our husband is a king in God's Kingdom and we have to smarten up and act like queens.

The King's Right-hand Woman

God in His wisdom knew it was not good for man to be alone. God knew man needed a companion, a helper, and a confidant. There are hundreds of books on marriage and a woman's biblical role, but I like to picture a woman as the king's right hand counselor. A king has the ultimate authority in decision-making. Often, he will have an advisor or aide, to whom he goes for advice. It is the advisor's duty to help the king accomplish his objectives. We have seen through history how advisors can so persuade authority that it has often led to the corruption and destruction of a kingdom. We can also see how good advice and influence can make it thrive.

I believe God created woman with the innate ability to influence the family. Using that influence wisely is a heavy responsibility. Some of us wives have a strong personality and it is very easy for us to give into the temptation to dominate our husbands, especially if they are not strong-willed or are very gracious by nature. Some of us may think we are smarter or wiser than our husbands, or we may have a low opinion of his ability to lead. Some of us may actually despise our husbands. We need to recognize this dangerous thinking. We must realize that when we think this way, we violate God's Laws and we subvert His purpose for marriage. We need to repent. If God has given us smarts or wisdom, we need to use it carefully and with humility and meekness. *Use it to inspire him to greatness.*

We have to change our attitudes about and perceptions of our husbands. We need to stop challenging their authority by trying to exert our own, but submit to them with strength and dignity. This does not mean we suddenly have no opinions or that we change our personality. It means learning to give our opinions and advice in a different way. Perhaps we suggest our ideas more often than exerting them or declaring them in his face. Sometimes we need to wait a while before blurting out everything that comes into our brains. (I am *never* guilty of this… yeah, right!)

The Bible tells us to "clothe yourselves instead with the beauty that comes from within, the unfading beauty of a gentle and quiet spirit, which is so precious to God" (1 Pet. 3:4). When we conduct ourselves in a manner that is gentle and meek, it is actually precious to God! It is also a more effective way to communicate in general. When speaking with anyone, people hear not just our words, but our attitude and demeanor. If we want to have an effect, we need to consider the way we communicate so that it doesn't put up walls. This is not manipulation; it is people skills. It is godliness.

In the story of Samson and Delilah, we see how a woman tried to influence her man by way of manipulation and nagging. The Bible tells us,

> With such nagging she prodded him day after day until he was tired to death. So he told her everything. "No razor has ever been used on my head," he said, "because I have been a Nazarite set apart to God since birth. If my head were shaved, my strength would leave me, and I would become as weak as any other man." (Judges 16:16–17)

How often do we do this? We nag, pester, and emotionally manipulate until we get our way. And if he just isn't "getting it," we think if we persist or make a bigger deal, then he will give in and we will get what we think we want. This method of course led to Samson's death and the death of many more. This is an ungodly approach to influence.

In contrast, look at how Esther handled herself. She gives us a wonderful example of how to influence a man—even a king. Two things come to mind: respect and food. A lot of food. Esther shows how a woman can be strong and bold, approaching her husband with important matters, even life-and-death issues, without insulting him or challenging his authority. Her spirit of humility so enchanted the king that he did not even seem to notice that she broke the court rule of approaching him without having first been beckoned. Her breaking the rule was bold on her part, but she had fasted and prayed. The Lord was with her. She prepared banquets and eased into her requests. She was not asking for some small favor either. She was asking him to revoke a decree that would annihilate the Jews and also condemn the king's own wife! She did not spring these things in his face. She did not nag or pester the king. Instead, with fasting and prayer, she approached him with a humble heart, respect and sincerity, always wanting to please him.

Esther was no doormat. She was wise. She was strategic with her requests and her manner of addressing her husband and king. The result: she saved her people.

We would be wise to follow Esther's example rather than Delilah's. It could make or break our effectiveness as godly women.

When we stand before God, we will be accountable for the type of influence we had in our homes. We will be accountable for how we treated these men God has chosen to lead us and our families. I love the story of Esther. Just think: if humble women can influence even kings, think of the potential influence ordinary mothers have on their children and how that ripples out into society. What we do with this role affects everything.

CHAPTER 5

Rugrat-Loosed and Fancy-Free

I don't know if this has happened to you, but it seems like I had unknowingly been brainwashed by our culture to believe that simply being a wife and mommy would never fulfill me completely. I struggled with feeling depressed at times because my friends were out traveling the world, getting degrees and living lives full of fun and adventure! Surely I could enjoy those things too if it weren't for…

In reality, many Christian women do experience years of "fun" and "adventure," full of singleness and independence. (If they only knew what an adventure it is to take several small children out to the grocery store!) While I am not knocking singleness *per se*, or fun or adventure or ambition (I am quite ambitious myself), the reality is that many women choose personal ambition in exchange for settling down—as if you can have only one or the other.

For example, Christian dating websites show there are an abundance of women between the ages of 25 and 40 with more degrees than a thermometer who have never been married or had kids. Some of us know women who seem to be having the times of their lives, pursuing careers and endless fun without a care in the world. They just can't be bothered with the thought of being tied down in a marriage, or, God forbid, those fat, booger-encrusted ankle-biters we call "children." These women prefer snot-free independence.

I am not talking about women who are called to be single, but about a completely different breed—Christian women who consciously *choose* singlehood. They are appearing more and more in the church. An interesting article on this worldwide movement appeared in *The New York Times* in 1998:

> Driven largely by prosperity and freedom, millions of women—here and throughout the developed world—are having fewer children than ever before. They stay in school longer, put more emphasis on work, and marry later. As a result, birth rates in many countries are now in a rapid, sustained decline. Never before—except in times of plague, war and deep economic depression—have birth rates fallen so low, for so long.[1]

The article surveyed a 33-year-old woman about her choice to not settle down and have a family. Like many women you and I know, she responded:

> There are times when I think perhaps I will be missing something important if I don't have a child . . . But today women finally have so many chances to have the life they want. To travel and work and learn. It's exciting and demanding. I just find it hard to see where the children would fit in.[2]

The article noted some serious implications for what seems to be a babyless movement across the globe:

> What was once regarded universally as a cherished goal—incredibly low birth rates—have in the industrial world suddenly become a cause for alarm. With life expectancy rising at the same time that fertility drops, most developed countries may soon find themselves with lopsided societies that will be nearly impossible to sustain: a large number of elderly and not enough young people working to support them. The change will affect every program—from health care and education to pension plans and military spending—that requires public funds. There is no longer a single country in Europe where people are having enough children to replace themselves when they die. Italy recently became the first nation in history where there are more people over the age of 60 than there are under the age of 20. This year Germany, Greece and Spain will probably all cross the same eerie divide.[3]

This is an alarming reality for America as well. This is our grandparents' reality, our parents' reality, and soon it will be our own reality. What kind of world will our children have to live in if we do not change this trend?

Think about this: the more the government has to step in where individuals, families, and churches have stepped out—like taking care of the elderly because there are not enough young people to do the job—the more heavily they will need to tax the people in order to meet the needs of the public.

God calls this slavery. High taxes and a government that takes care of everybody is also a government that takes away freedom in exchange for those things. That is why it is slavery. God required only 10% of our income. Our government demands double, triple and in some areas more than that!

This is tyranny: When the State demands more than what God has required and usurps jurisdiction in an area where God has not given it. Often it begins with our money—taxing us for all these "good programs"—but there is no end after that. What was once the responsibility of individual citizens and the church (taking care of the poor, the elderly, raising funds for anything that was needed within a community), has now been passed onto the State—all because we're not having enough babies who are being brought up to take responsibility as their forefathers did.

Who would have thought that not having babies would lead to slavery? Many of us have not given it thought. In addition, consider the fact that the average American and Canadian Christian family has a birthrate of 1.9 and the average Muslim family has a birthrate of 6. Within a couple generations, a religion very hostile to Christianity will dominate several countries in the world. We have not been thinking about those things, have we? Nevertheless, pastor and author Voddie Baucham explains a real need:

> Who's going to fix our ethical, spiritual, economic, and political crisis in the next generation if those of us who know the answer (the Gospel) shut it down and stop launching arrows [children] simply because they may require a little financial sacrifice in the short run?[4]

The recent documentary *Demographic Winter* looks deeper into the social impact and consequences of decreasing birthrates. It demonstrates how this epidemic will affect our world as never before in history. The sexual revolution of the '60s, higher incomes, the no-fault divorce allowances, high percentages of cohabiting couples, the birth control pill, and feminism all play a large role in this. Beyond these factors, the church has generally been silent on the topic. Can you remember the last time you heard a sermon on how you and your husband need to "get to work" and be fruitful? For the most part, it seems our worldly culture is having more impact on us in this department than our church. That is backward.

THE END OF AN ERA

I considered another sad fact. When the feminists—many of whom have aborted their children and refused to settle down and have a family—die, everything their parents poured into them—all the efforts, labors, and toils of the hundreds of generations before them—will die with them. They have ended a part of history. Their bloodline stops there forever. How tragic. The other ironic thing about this is that many of these feminists do not realize that when they fight for abortion, they ultimately fight to kill themselves right out of history. Because these women are ripping babies from the womb and fighting for this "right," they bring an end to not only their bloodline, but also their false ideologies and anti-Christian views and actions. How tragic also that some Christian men and women choose the same path as their secular adversaries.

Let me be clear: I don't think it is a sin for Christian women to pursue their dreams, travel, or get degrees. However, I wish we had all been taught to consider the fact that when we die, we take all that education, all the memories of travels, all our ambitions and dreams to the grave. If all we pursue in life is our own selfish goals and wants, what we leave behind is absolutely nothing. There is no legacy—nothing of value to pass to a future generation. Maybe we affected a few people around us in our circle of friends or family, but they too will take any impact we had on them to the grave. Current generations are not future generations. Children are. *Children are the future.*

Christian families having kids are the *means* by which God chooses to "subdue the earth." Subdue means to bring into submission. It means dominion, not *domination*. It also means stewardship—which means Christians taking responsibility for everything that goes on in the earth. It is the Great Commission—it is making disciples of all nations, starting with our own children. We begin by creating a godly culture within the home, and that will eventually spread out into the community and beyond.

I'd like to add here that when it comes to the subject of having kids, the Bible doesn't give us an exact number that we're supposed to shoot for. It doesn't speak about birth control, the different scientific methods used to prevent an egg from attaching to the uterine lining, the controversy about it, or how each family should approach family planning. The one thing the Bible does say is that we are to *multiply and fill the earth*. This should be a no-brainer for us. We should look at children as a wonderful thing and should strive to have them if possible. The topic of birth control is so highly controversial and debated within conservative Christian circles that it has our heads spinning! Many of us have different convictions about this. I am not here to push my conviction in this matter, as I believe this comes down to a stewardship issue and each family must answer to God for their decision. All I want to do is encourage myself and others to think of children as God thinks of them: a blessing, not a curse.

What bothers me most is that much of the church has adopted a worldly attitude about having kids. Most of the time pastors never tell us what the Bible says about covenantal blessings and generational progress through godly seed. Even if they were to preach on this more often, we are so addicted to materialism and the prosperity of our day that we actually prefer having *stuff* to having children! It's not that we *can't* have children—it's that we *won't*!

This has never happened before in history. It's sad that we sacrifice the possibility of a large family on the Ikea altar of "better" living. We want bigger vehicles and fewer people to fill them. We want more *square feet* with fewer *actual feet* padding around in them. We're addicted to comfort, convenience, and self-centered pursuits instead of Kingdom pursuits.

It's not uncommon when a family walks into a church with more than four children and everyone gasps, as though this is a wonder. "How could you have all those kids?" "Haven't you figured out what causes that?" "How can you afford them?" "Why?" "What do you mean, you homeschool them?" "Aren't you worried about socialization?" "Who says you're qualified to teach them?"

Many of us ask these same questions because we've adopted the thinking of the world—that having many kids equals poverty, inconvenience, and unhappiness. We have all been automated to believe that comfort comes first and if you want to have a good life, two kids is the maximum, preferably a boy and a girl. Anything more than that is, by the world's standard, "irresponsible." A website actually gave one hundred reasons *not* to have kids. Here are a few. Notice that every single reason is all about "me" and stems from pure selfishness:

1. You will be happier and less likely to suffer from depression.
2. Childless marriages are happier.
3. You will have the capacity and time for meaningful, engaged, quality adult relationships.
4. You will be able to save for a comfortable retirement.
5. You are more likely to be an engaged and involved aunt or uncle because you are not jaded and worn down by your own kids.
6. You can fully pursue and develop your career.
7. You can fully pursue your educational goals.
8. You can decorate your home as you wish with as many beautiful and/or breakable things as you wish and you will not have to child-proof your house.
9. Your house will be free of junky, plastic "kindercrap."
10. Your spouse will get all the love and attention he/she deserves. You will come first in your spouse/partner's life.[5]

Many Christian women actually reason like some of these unbelieving women to justify not having kids. Worldly reasoning is not acceptable for any Christian. Children are not a burden. God tells us to have them and to multiply. You do the math. I also want to add that I don't believe a family is any less spiritual if they can't have children, or don't have twelve children like some families whom I do admire! Our pastor has reminded us that quivers come in different sizes and look different in each family, so we shouldn't guilt or put pressure on each other.

Priorities

After I came to these realizations, I wondered how a woman with a lot of ambition or a gifting is supposed to embrace the role of wife and mother and not feel ripped off somehow. At first, I thought I might have to give up my dreams altogether if I were really going to be that Proverbs 31 wife we all hear about. I always wanted to be a professional songwriter. I have an entrepreneur side. I have this *thing* and that *thing* I want to accomplish. Would I really have to lay it all down? Well, perhaps for a while, until I found contentment and satisfaction in my primary role, the most important role on earth.

I also knew that when the time was right, and when I had my priorities in order and found joy in doing that, God would provide a way for me to function in my other gifts and pursue those without compromising my family. That is exactly what has happened. I signed on with a music development company that only required I come in to work on my album once a week for a few hours—hardly the life of a professional musician on tour without their family!

Life with several busy little ones is a challenge, so I pursue only one or two outside activities or hobbies at a time. Right now, it's my health (I'm expecting number four at the time of this writing) and finishing my music album. Anything else on the plate is too much and I find myself easily overwhelmed. My advice for young wives and moms who have gusto to do *stuff*: get your priorities in order first. Don't do anything else until you are totally joyful in your role. Then pick one pursuit. Make sure your husband supports you 100%, and then don't abuse that privilege. After God, marriage comes first. Nothing should compromise that.

When I stopped worrying so much about accomplishing all of my personal pursuits at the same time, life was much happier. Of course, I'm doing something much more important than making an album or writing. When I make breakfast for my family, do the laundry (Lord, help me with that!), and read to my little ones—*with a dominion perspective*—I am investing in future generations. I leave something that will never die. I am investing in the souls of my children, and there is nothing more precious than that.

God tells parents that if we do our part in training and discipling our children in the ways of the Lord, we can stand on His promise that "when they are old, they will not depart from it." That is a motivator for me to get in gear and discipline and instruct them in the way my Father's Word has instructed me.

Lastly, I would like to encourage you to create a mission statement for yourself. I have recognized one thing—when I fail to maintain personal self-discipline and a household routine, chaos ensues and I lose control with my parenting. Before I know it, the house is in disarray, the kids are disobedient and bouncing off the walls and I'm frazzled at every end. In my own mind, I become the epitome of what feminists look at and say, "You see that stressed-out, frumpy mom? That's why I chose a career instead of kids."

So in order to keep my sanity and really bring focus to what I'm doing day-in and day-out, I made a mission statement. I have it printed out and I keep it on the fridge and in my planning binder where I have to see it all the time. It's an ongoing work in progress, but as of now, it looks something like this:

MY LIFE'S MISSION STATEMENT

Wife:

1. Be the best helper to Steve I can possibly be.
2. Serve, respect, and appreciate him.
3. Speak in a voice he loves to hear, serve him food he loves to eat, and welcome him with a warm embrace.
4. Be what he looks forward to at the end of the day.
5. Be a good steward of my health and don't "let myself go."

Mother:

6. Raise kids who know God and love His Law/Grace.
7. Have vision and purpose in moment-to-moment parenting.
8. Be more loving, more in control of myself, more patient and purposeful.
9. Be a better problem-solver.
10. Raise kids well-rounded in trades, skills, language, arts, music, apologetics, theology, science, business, economics, etc.
11. Have more fun and *be* more fun.

Disciple/Student:

12. Continue self-discipline to read and learn something new every day.

13. Be faithful to re-examine myself and ask God to refine my imperfections and defects.
14. Run this earthly race with more purpose, vision, passion, and ambition.
15. Pass down everything I learn to my kids, grandkids, and beyond: verbally, written, and in other forms of media—to be passed on and kept in the family for generations.

Musician/Entrepreneur:

16. Fully develop and access my musical and song-writing ability.
17. Create a product that will return all investments and make a profit.
18. "Work" from home and help ease Steve's financial load.
19. Ultimate goal: to create enough wealth to buy land and other hard assets and pass it down to our descendants.

Yours does not have to be that long. It could be just a simple sentence or phrase; but the point is to define your goal and purpose right now in your role. When you do this, it keeps you from running around like a chicken with your head cut off. It promotes a focus, a conscious effort, accountability and personal responsibility to God. You might be surprised how good it feels to make yourself a mission statement. Put it somewhere you will be sure to see it. Commitment to rethinking our attitudes toward our husbands, our attitudes toward children, and our role in society is a giant step to changing the world!

CHAPTER 6

Pills & Bifocals

If you are a wife or a mom, you are God's weapon for mass *reconstruction*! As the decay of a secular society continues to set in, and as it continually collapses, the best part is that God has a plan to rebuild the nations. This happens through us—the family! This is why God wants us to multiply. While we are constantly evangelizing and discipling the pagan nations, we are also growing our own Christian nations—right out of our wombs! The family is God's weapon for victory on earth.

We looked at some of our wrong attitudes concerning children in the previous chapter. Now let's look at God's view of children:

> *Be fruitful and increase in number and fill the earth.* (Genesis 9:1)

> *Children are a heritage of the Lord, the fruit of the womb is His reward. As arrows are in the hand of a mighty man; so are children of the youth. Happy is the man that has his quiver full of them . . .* (Psalm 127:3–5)

> *. . . She is thy companion, and the wife of thy covenant. And did not He make you one? . . . And why one? That He may seek a godly seed.* (Malachi 2:14–15)

> *Thy wife shall be as a fruitful vine by the sides of thine house; thy children like olive plants round about thy table . . .* (Psalm 128:3)

The first command God gave to Adam and Eve and to Noah after the Flood was to "increase in number and fill the earth." This command has not gone away. Over-population is a myth! Whenever we hear things about that, we have to compare it to what God commands first and foremost. We saw in the previous chapter that if anything, we have a population that's declining like never before in history. God's plan always wins over what scientists or the media tells us. God says, "Have lots of children." Why? What is God after? *Godly offspring!* (Mal. 2:15).

Now why is it a big deal that we have godly offspring? God says, "Like arrows in the hand of a warrior are the children of one's youth. Blessed is the man who fills his quiver with them! He shall not be put to shame when he speaks with his enemies in the gate" (Ps. 127:4–5).

A godly family who multiplies is *God's weapon for victory*. Our children are arrows (or in modern technology—ballistic missiles) being launched at the enemy from our homes. Kelly Crawford, in her blog *Generation Cedar*, presented her point well:

> "Like arrows in the hand of a mighty warrior, so are the children of one's youth."
>
> *Why?*
>
> They shall speak with the enemies in the gate.
>
> *Why?*
>
> Because "Thou shalt have no other gods before me."
>
> And that commandment was not a personal one. It was spoken to a nation, and still is. Our problem? We make everything personal. We don't understand God's sovereign [purpose] as it relates to the *big* picture. As it relates to having children, we assess our personal situation, and decide that God couldn't possibly mean us. It's so not about whether I can afford to send them to college, or buy them a car, or let them all play sports. And while God is immensely concerned with our personal lives (don't get me wrong), He is even *more* concerned with fulfilling His Kingdom purposes. And how does He do that? One way is through His people! And practically speaking, through numbers. We no longer live in a Christian nation. And it is an abomination. Why are the enemies of God prevailing? Because the people of God are not raising up warriors to "contend with them at the gates." We are committing the blasphemous sin of tolerating every religion that walks through the gates in the name of love. Our methodologies are not working. We have more programs, more money, more evangelical tools now than ever before in history. Yet the spiritual temperature of this country continues to decline.[1]

So if we understand that God has commanded us to "increase in number" and raise "arrows" that He will use for His Kingdom purposes, we need to better define how we should do that. Seems like an overwhelming task if we have to figure it out moment by moment. The good news is that God already has a plan and a strategy for a glorious outcome!

The Red Pill or The Blue Pill?

What is the ultimate goal of parenting? Your answer to this question will alter your corner of history. What you think determines your actions. Is it our job as parents to simply love our kids? Is it to raise "responsible, courteous citizens"? Is it to do our very best and hope they don't get pregnant, fall into drug activity, or worse? Is it to hope that they take on the religion of their parents so they can be like us?

We just touched on the point that God commands us to multiply and launch arrows. Our family is a weapon God will use against the enemy. Every warrior or soldier goes through crucial training for the battlefield. They learn discipline, strategy, emergency response, combat, adaptation, and more. They develop mental capacity and physical skill. Mental training is a very big aspect of being a warrior. Having wimps on the battlefield could mean losing the war.

In the case of raising a new army for Christ, the training begins at birth and ends, for the most part, when they leave our home to be married. We have approximately eighteen to twenty years to make such an impact on these little people that it will alter the course of history in one way or another.

It all begins with how we mould their worldview, which I will explain. If you get one thing out of this book, I hope it is this: *there is no such thing as neutral*. God is not neutral. Satan is not neutral. The world is not neutral.

We have all heard the saying, "Ideas have consequences." It is vital that we understand why that is true if we're going to change the world. The basic premise is that ideas shape the world because ideas shape people. This concept will be a theme throughout the rest of this book. We constantly interpret facts and information based on the system of thought we have adopted—whether we know it or not.

There is a constant clash of God's system versus the world's system. The world is run by a certain ideology. God has His own. The world's system is in active opposition to God's system of thought, and it imposes its own system of thought under the name "neutrality." Satan wants us to believe that when we watch the news, "it is neutral." When we read the newspaper, "it is neutral." When we send our kids to public school, "it is neutral." This is a complete lie! It is the ultimate wolf parading around in sheep's clothing.

The only way to combat Satan's counterfeit system of thought is to make sure we are interpreting facts and information *God's way*—through God's world order or system of thought. This is a Christian worldview—*to have the mind of Christ*. The Bible says, "Do not conform to the pattern of this world, but be transformed by the renewing of your mind. Then you will be able to test and approve what God's will is—His good, pleasing, and perfect will" (Rom. 2:12).

We cannot discern what the will of God is if our minds operate like the world's. How shocking to think that we have saved souls, but pagan brains!

Many of us have become "moralists." We are converted but change only our behavior. We stop doing bad things, sure, but many of us who were taught by the world's system (we'll call it "Caesar") still think like Caesar and not like Christ! We are mistaken if we think that our change of lifestyle is enough to change the world. Pastor Dennis Peacock pointed out this very thing:

> If you think that because Christians don't drink, or drink moderately, that it's somehow going to be a witness to the world, give yourself a break. We cannot compete with Islam relative to abstinence from alcohol. If you think sexual purity is going to convince the world, then you don't understand Hinduism. If you think treating our families right is going to convert the world, you don't understand Mormonism. Whatever thing we think is going to convert or convince the world, largely the world could care less because they've seen all that in one form or another.[2]

Moralism or good behavior, as Christian as it might be, is not enough to change the world. We have to change our entire strategy! We need to change the way we interpret every single piece of information that comes into our brains and spirits. We need to realize that if we grew up in the world's school system, Caesar taught us our history. Caesar taught us math, art, music, and logic. Behind the "facts" was an entire biased system of thought. Without even knowing it, we adopted Caesar's whole system of thought. We were being conformed to the pattern of Caesar, ever so subtly. History is not what Caesar says it is. Music, art, and literature are not what Caesar says they are. To understand history, music, and art the way God says it really is, we must transform our minds to the image of Christ.

This does not happen automatically when we become Christians. God calls us to personal responsibility through obedience. When we begin to undo the work of the enemy by becoming obedient to Christ—taking every thought captive to Him—we are now a total threat to the enemy and world system. We have officially taken the red pill and jumped out of "the Matrix" of false neutrality. No longer are we dancing to the tune of Satan's system. We are dancing to the Almighty's tune and it is taking us to a completely new level of authority and dominion.

Let's briefly examine what is behind every worldview. Remember: even people who don't realize it do believe something in one form or another when it comes to these questions.

A worldview is *the set of underlying beliefs a person has about the world that governs his or her daily actions and decisions.* It is like wearing glasses. Everyone wears a pair of worldview glasses which determine how they see the big picture in life. It is essentially a view of these fundamental questions:

View of God:	Is there one? Many? What is He like… personal or impersonal?
View of Man:	Where did we come from? Why are we here? Is man God? Is man equal to God or on his way to equality?
View of Truth:	Is there such a thing as absolute truth? How do we determine what is true?
View of Knowledge:	How do we know things? Is the material world and our five senses the be-all and end-all?
View of Ethics:	Is there any absolute standard of ethics (right and wrong), or are ethics relative and/or situational?

Even if you've never asked yourself those questions, you already have a view about them. Even if you don't realize it, your answers affect your everyday decisions. Throughout this book, I hope you will begin to see how your worldview affects everything from how you plan, how you save or spend your money, how you educate your kids, how you view your marriage, house chores, and even the importance you put in health! Because of this, it affects how you will change the world, for better or for worse.

Worldview Lenses

When we initially mention the big topics that are included in a worldview, some of us parents may think we should leave that stuff for when our kids are older, since right now they are still trying to grasp the meaning of the words, "Please don't try to flush your sister down the toilet."

The reality is that every day our kids witness their parents' every word and action—and the experience they have tells them something about the nature of reality, God, man, sin, redemption, and eternity. By a few years old, toddlers have already organized ideas into patterns. They have integrated the information they have received in their brains to make "sense" of things. As a result, they are capable of understanding some very deep concepts, even if they don't ever verbalize it. It is why we must instill in them a distinctly Christian worldview from birth onward. They take in everything around them and it results in planting roots, for better or worse.

My three year old knows and understands the basic concept of sin. She knows that she is a sinner and that we are all born into sin. She knows she needs forgiveness and needs to repent to the Almighty. She understands her purpose in life is "to glorify God and to enjoy Him forever."

We had some help with teaching her this. We use this little book of questions and answers for children that help to teach them basic doctrine. The fancy word for it is a "catechism." In the olden days, most Christian homes used this method to help little children properly memorize and understand the basic doctrines of Christianity. "Catechizing" your kids is a very easy but proactive way of helping them understand many Christian truths that much of today's church is without.

And to think, my three year old understands things that some pastors do not! We make it a lot of fun and use animations and gestures while we recite the questions and answers. Our little ones are not some kind of model kids, believe me. We all have seen the reality of rottenness in our children—sometimes when they are only six months old!

But just to give you an idea of what children are capable of, my two older kids—at the ages of three and almost five—have memorized the Ten Commandments (and understand what they mean), Psalm 1, Psalm 23, Psalm 110, and the Lord's Prayer. I'm sure there are children who have memorized much more.

This is not tooting anyone's horn or setting a bar. It is simply an example of how amazingly receptive their brains are! I find that if I make up little actions and animations in my voice, it is more fun and it seems to stick very quickly.

Some of you are thinking, "What's the point? They are too young to really grasp what all that scripture means." I have thought about that myself and believe their spirits understand what their minds cannot. Even if they don't fully grasp it all now, memorizing the Word ministers to their spirits and sets down those roots.

When they are very little, they don't understand why we buckle them in their car seats or why they cannot stick their hand in a blender. We know as parents what it is for and how it could save their lives. The same principle applies here with teaching them core doctrine and Scripture: when the world surrounds them with false ideas, it could save their lives!

Learning to memorize the Word of God is a part of their young worldview training. They will memorize and memorize. They will ask questions and we will have answers. They will learn the basics. We will help them to pray and be in the presence of God daily. This foundation will grow deep, deep roots. This will anchor them for the rest of their lives. We are not parenting by the seat of our pants; we are proactive parents with a big picture in mind. God tells us to do all this in Deuteronomy 6:6–9:

> *And these words which I command you today shall be in your heart. You shall teach them diligently to your children, and shall talk of them when*

you sit in your house, when you walk by the way, when you lie down, and when you rise up. You shall bind them as a sign on your hand, and they shall be as frontlets between your eyes. You shall write them on the doorposts of your house and on your gates.

When they are a little older, we will delve into the Word at a more complex level. But underneath these things, they will already have a Christian worldview by which they will be able to judge and discern all other things. They will have an ultimate standard.

You see, the problem is that when we went to school, they told us only *what* to think. Did you know you could be the smartest, most educated person, and not know *how* to think? That is the majority of Christians today. There's a reason why they don't teach logic in public schools anymore. If students learned how to think, they might not accept what the school teaches. We are going to change that for ourselves right now and we are going to change that for our children. *That* will revolutionize our whole world.

We will teach our children what God has to say about every subject we can think of. The Bible is the answer to all of life's problems. It addresses everything either specifically or through principle. We will protect our children, not shelter them. Sheltering is keeping them from knowing what really goes on in the world. Protecting our kids means we equip them with the *discernment* of God as they mature and prove personal self-discipline and wisdom.

We continually dress them in the armor of God until they can dress themselves. There is a difference between foolishly sheltering and biblically protecting. If we never allow children to see or know of anything bad or questionable in the world, it will not promote maturity in them. What it promotes is ignorance, and then often rebellion. Many of us have seen good Christian kids go off the deep end when they reach independence—and maybe we were those kids! This is because they were never shown how to handle the reality of the world from a biblical point of view. They weren't taught maturity in increments they could handle.

Our kids need to understand the world around us is fallen in every way and that it is our job as Christians to bring the Gospel into every crack and sphere and redeem it for His glory. We can do this when we watch a movie together as a family or spot a homosexual couple on the street. They need to understand how to think about it in God's terms and then how to act upon what they have understood.

Because they are so impressionable, we must also take into consideration now every influence over our children inevitably affects their worldview. Anytime someone baby-sits them, they are affected. The friends we allow affect them. The movies they watch affect them. The examples they see in us as parents affect them. Who is their teacher? Who wrote the book they are reading? What kind of external worldviews are shaping them without our knowledge? Are they godly influences? Does it line up with Deuteronomy 6:6–9? Whose glasses are they wearing—God's glasses or the world's glasses? Do our kids wear bifocals—a little bit of Christianity and a little bit of the world?

It is our job to make sure they get the purest lenses possible while they are under our roof so they can see clearly for the rest of their lives.

It is because we finally realized the importance of taking the red pill, getting out of the Matrix of neutrality and wearing God's glasses in life that my husband and I are living every day intentionally and purposefully for our children, grandchildren, and beyond. We realize that we must live out our marriage and our parenting with the big picture in mind always. We must ask the question—how is what we are doing now going to change the future and affect future generations?

I would like to encourage you to ask the same question. On those days when you find yourself overwhelmed or unsatisfied because of your role, consider the big picture. Consider the lasting impact of a mother and father who teach their kids how to bring Christ into every sphere of life. Consider what instilling a biblical worldview will do for the country! Consider the effect of a household that believes Christ is reigning *now*—not in the distant future—instead of a household that believes He has ultimately failed in history.

By the way, great godly men and women—the ones that changed the course of history—didn't just appear out of thin air. They came about as the result of faithful generations before them: moms and dads who taught their children the ways of the Lord, diligently and fervently.

CHAPTER 7

God's Law for ~~Dummies~~ Mommies

Hang on! This chapter might make you a little uncomfortable. We are about to look at some common misconceptions about God's Word. If you are ready for that kind of challenge, read on! We will address God's promises for our kids—the assurance we can rest on—but also what God requires of us. There are parts that might feel tricky, or it might challenge what you grew up believing, but hang in there. It's so liberating when you understand God's intentions and overall picture.

Here is a huge promise God has given parents:

> But the steadfast love of the LORD is from everlasting to everlasting on those who fear him, and His righteousness to children's children, to those who keep His covenant and remember to do His commandments. (Psalm 103:17–18)

This verse is all about God's plan to save our kids down through the multi-generational line. Whoa! The word "multi-generation" isn't a word we hear often, but it's one that God uses all the time in different ways. He doesn't just think of saving one person here and one person there, although He does do that. God's full intention is to save entire generations down the line!

We have a promise, but we have a contingency—an act of obedience and response on our part. While the salvation of our children is ultimately in the hands of God who "foreknew" (which means to fore-*love*) and predestined His people (Rom. 8:29), Psalm 103 tell us we have every reason to expect our children will come to salvation if we obey God's instructions for us as parents. It's a promise, and there's a condition attached to that promise. God never attaches a condition that He does not first give us the grace to carry out.

This must be our first prayer. We ought to pray for the grace to obey. Alone in our depravity, we would not be able to do it. When God gives us a specific command, He changes our hearts and makes us able to do what we could not do on our own.

The first requirement is that we fear God. We must submit to Him completely. We must understand His hatred toward sin. We must fear His judgment—even as believers.

We have often made God into our "buddy Jesus" and have forgotten how unfathomably huge and mighty He is—He created the universe! We have not discovered even a fraction of the expanse He has formed. Jesus is our friend, but He is the King of all kings—and He shall be feared!

Don't get me wrong, Jesus is our friend, but remember that Jesus identified Himself as the "I Am." The same "I Am" that revealed Himself to Moses in the burning bush. This means Jesus is God. Our sweet, precious Jesus is the same God who slaughtered the foes of the Israelites. Our wonderful friend Jesus is the same God who sent fire and brimstone on Sodom and Gomorrah. How's that for a mind bender?

Jesus is our friend, to be sure. He is on His people's side; He is not our enemy. But let us not forget that He is the High King and Almighty as well. We should fear Him. This means with both reverence and real heart-pounding fear! If we don't have either of those, we don't understand who God is.

God's second requirement of us as parents is to keep His covenant. God originally made a covenant with Abraham:

> *And I will establish my covenant between me and you and your offspring after you throughout their generations for an everlasting covenant, to be God to you and to your offspring after you.* (Genesis 17:7)

We seldom hear about the vast significance of this promise for us today. Who are Abraham's offspring? All believers. The promise is that He will be our God and our children's God. When Psalm 103 says to "keep His covenant," it simply means to trust in God's promise. Romans 4:3 tells us the only thing Abraham did that was counted unto him as righteous was that he "believed God." It is faith. However, obedience and the fruit of that obedience always accompany faith. We have to trust that God will keep His promises to us as parents.

God's third requirement is that we follow through with our belief and trust and actually do His commandments. Jesus summed it up when He said:

> *"Love the Lord your God with all your heart and with all your soul and with all your mind." This is the first and greatest commandment. And the second is like it: "Love your neighbor as yourself." All the Law and the Prophets hang on these two commandments.* (Matthew 22:37–40)

Jesus was quoting Deuteronomy 6:5. "You shall love the Lord your God with all your heart and with all your soul and with all your might," and

Leviticus 19:18. "You shall not take vengeance, nor bear any grudge against the sons of your people, but you shall love your neighbor as yourself."

Jesus is simplifying things for us dummies. He's saying the Ten Commandments summarize the hundreds of Mosaic laws God gave in the Old Testament. The two commands summarize the Ten Commandments to make it even more simple. God requires that we still remember and keep His commandments today, even in the New Covenant. We know this because Jesus made it crystal clear:

> *Do not think that I have come to abolish the Law or the Prophets; I have not come to abolish them but to fulfill them. For truly, I say to you,* **until heaven and earth pass away, not an iota, not a dot, will pass from the Law until all is accomplished***. Therefore whoever relaxes one of the least of these commandments and teaches others to do the same will be called least in the kingdom of heaven, but whoever does them and teaches them will be called great in the kingdom of heaven.* (Matthew 5:17–19. Emphasis mine.)

Is the Law Done Away With Now?

When Jesus says He came not to abolish, but to fulfill the Law and Prophets, what does that mean? I used to read that verse and think the word "fulfill" meant "abolish." That is obviously not what Jesus is saying because He clarifies He is not abolishing the Law. What Jesus meant was that He is the only one able to keep the Law perfectly. He is able to obey it to a "T" because He is sinless (2 Cor. 5:21). No one ever has or ever will be able to fulfill the Law perfectly because all are sinners and fall short. Jesus would do that which we could not. In His perfection, He fulfilled the Law and Prophets. Then Jesus says a serious thing: not even the smallest stroke of a letter will pass from the Law until He settles all things at the end of history. So if we teach our children that God's commandments are not for today, God will call us "the least in the kingdom of heaven." Ouch!

Some of us have heard—and maybe even preached—that the Old Testament doesn't apply in the New Testament, but when we read Jesus' words, we see that is definitely not true! There is an easy way to figure out what applies and doesn't apply in the Old Testament. The whole Bible is the Word of God, not just the New Testament. Unless Jesus' death, resurrection, and ascension actually changed the application of a law, it still stands today. For example, we no longer need animal sacrifices or a temple because Jesus was the true living sacrifice and every believer's body is now a temple (1 Cor.

6:19). Circumcision is no longer required because God circumcises our hearts. All the ceremonial laws represented what was to come in the New Covenant: the real thing! The law still stands, but it has been kept in Christ for New Covenant believers. What remains for us now are all God's moral laws. God's laws prohibiting idolatry, adultery, and stealing are still applied the same way today.

If we try that the other way around—abolishing all the Old Testament laws unless it is specifically mentioned in the New Testament—we end up with some serious problems. The New Testament does not mention many sins—like bestiality, for example. Does that mean bestiality is okay in the New Covenant? Obviously not. This is why the whole book is the full Word of God. We also know the importance of the Old Testament because 2 Timothy 3:16–17 tells us, "*All* Scripture is breathed out by God and profitable for teaching, for reproof, for correction, and for training in righteousness, that the man of God may be competent, equipped for every good work."

Keep in mind that the New Testament was not around yet. While this verse applies to the entire Bible now, at the time, it concerned the only Scripture that was known or available at the time—the Old Testament.

How many of us commonly hear, "We're not under law anymore, we're under grace"? The truth is that believers are and have always been under *both*. You cannot have one without the other.

In the Old Testament, people were still saved by grace through faith. It is not as though the Law saved people in the Old Testament but it switched to Grace in the New Testament. No, God always saved people by His grace. The Law was there to protect them and reveal their sin. God put the sacrificial system in place so they could have a relationship with Him until He sent Jesus as the perfect sacrifice. Paul reminds us of this, "Do we then nullify the Law through faith? May it never be! On the contrary, we establish the Law" (Rom. 3:21). In an article for American Vision, author Gary DeMar wrote:

> No one ever was or ever will be saved by keeping the law. This is the Bible's point when Romans 6:14 says that the Christian is not under the law. This is far different from saying that the Christian is not obligated to obey the law as a standard of righteousness.[1]

When it comes to the character and nature of God, we know He is the same yesterday, today, and forever. His morality never changes. It transcends all space and time. Stealing will be wrong until the end of time. Adultery and worshiping false gods will be forever wrong. You see, the commandments are simply a reflection of God's character. It tells us about His perfect nature. It tells us how He feels, how He is grieved or brought to anger over sin—which is simply anything contrary to His nature.

When we teach our children what the commandments are and how to obey them, we teach them about God Himself. We show them His gracious mercy. If God didn't love us, He would not have given us laws. He would not have given us restrictions and boundaries. He would have let us run loose and drive ourselves into destruction and damnation.

But the Law is what gives us the ability to discern good from evil. It is our yardstick—our ultimate standard for truth. Without an ultimate standard of truth, anyone can claim something is right or wrong. Or they can claim good and evil do not exist. I've met plenty of those people. They believe that, though, only until someone hurts or offends *them*... then suddenly there's right and wrong!

We also need to realize that in loving our children the way God commanded us to, it is not about making a mini-me. It's not about duplicating ourselves. It's all about Jesus and conforming to the image of God. It's not even about our personal relationship with them, although God chooses to work in their lives *through* our relationships. It's all about God's relationship with our kids. We love our kids on behalf of God. We teach them to love and obey Biblical commands on behalf of God. We are officially their foster parents. They do not belong to us. They are not our property. They are God's property. God grants us temporary custody for a temporary training time on earth, for His purposes. This is why it is such a serious responsibility that we disciple them properly, the way He wants it done. When we teach them and disciple them in this way it gives them a sense of true belonging and identity. God is saying to them through us, "You are mine. Love me, serve me, learn my ways, and learn my Law. Be upholders of my ways and walk with me." We hold them accountable to the covenant. They must know and feel God's love. God never tires of saying "I love you" and so we must never tire of saying it to our kids. We have to express it to them by demonstrating it word and deed. Hug them every day. When we embrace them, they should know and feel they are receiving the embrace of the Father.

When parents fear the Lord, when we believe the promise that He will be our God and our children's God, when we act on it by obeying His commandments—teaching our children obedience also—we can rest, knowing that God has the salvation of our children in His hands and will fulfill His promise to a thousand generations.

CHAPTER 8

The Idle Mind is Whose Playground?

If you thought the last chapter was intense, wait until you read this one! Warning: if you are like I was a few years ago, you might be tempted to throw the book out because of this one topic. I want to encourage you: if you have gotten this far, you are definitely serious about changing your life and changing the world. You are on the path to making it your mission in life to do things God's way. Don't stop now…keep on reading. If you don't burn this book after this chapter, it might change the lives of all your future descendants!

How else do we disciple our children in the way they should go? A very important—yet controversial—aspect is the way we educate our kids. By now I'm sure you can tell I'm not too faint-hearted when it comes to talking about controversial topics within Christianity. In the minds of our children is where the battle really lies.

We've all heard the expression "the idle mind is the devil's playground." From kindergarten through grade twelve, the average student spends more than 14,000 seat hours learning someone's ideologies about the world. This is why the Bible equates education with discipleship. The Bible does not mention the specific word "school." That is because the Bible knows nothing of such things. Schooling is a modern concept. But the "training of the mind" is as old as time. The Bible addresses very strongly the issue of how we are to train our minds and our children's minds. Learning math and science and art is training or educating the mind. They are the same in God's eyes. Noah Webster's 1828 dictionary defines *educate* in this way:

> To bring up, as a child; to instruct; to inform and enlighten the understanding; to instill into the mind principles of arts, science, morals, religion and behavior. To educate children well is one of the most important duties of parents and guardians.[1]

This definition is a biblical definition. It sure sounds like discipleship, doesn't it? "To instill in the mind…" That is specifically why Jesus said, "A student is not above his teacher, but everyone who is fully trained will be like his teacher" (Luke 6:40).

The Bible says our children *will be like their teachers* and God requires us to disciple and instruct them in the ways of the Lord. There is only one kind of education our kids should get: a distinctly Christian, Bible-based education.

Don't throw this book out yet! I don't know where you are in your understanding, but frankly, until about four years ago I didn't give a flying hoot about public versus Christian education or home schooling. Until I realized the seriousness of the whole issue, I thought it was a matter of "personal conviction." I pretty much assumed that each individual should just pray and think about it—as if it were some kind of mystical decision. Well, I'd like to share some of the reasons that truly convinced me that a secular, government education is not an option for Christian parents—not now, not ever.

1. *You shall not steal.* (Exodus 20:15)

At first, this might seem strange that I quote one of the Ten Commandments to argue for a Christian education, but let's look a little closer at this. Earlier we saw how important it is to God that we still obey His commands in the New Covenant and how Jesus defined love as obedience to them (John 14:15).

The public education system starts on the wrong foot because it breaks the eighth commandment regarding stealing. The way it works is that the government takes money from people by force to pay for the education of other people's children. There are serious penalties if you don't pay up—like losing your property. This is stealing in its very basic form. The government is certainly not above God's Law! It is to submit to it. This might raise all kinds of objections in your mind initially, but please hear me out.

Let me put it another way. If my neighbor to the left is poor and my neighbor to the right is rich, and I go the rich house and take money to give to my poor neighbor, regardless of my good intention, that is called stealing. It violates God's Law. In today's society, the consequence would be imprisonment. If I hire my friend to go and rob the house so we can give it to our poor neighbor, it is still stealing. We will both go to jail for conspiracy, breaking and entering, and theft. Now purportedly, when I elect the civil government to go ahead and take money from people so it can fund things like public schools and programs for the poor, somehow that is no longer stealing. Something has gone awry! Here is the real question: is it okay for the government to take money from people when it's "for a good cause"? The answer does not lie with how we feel about it. The answer lies with how God feels about it. You might be thinking, "Well, how will children get educated if the government doesn't pay for the schooling?"

There are a couple of points to think about here. For one, the education children receive from government schools is resulting in the highest illiteracy rates in modern history! Many students graduate and cannot read. This is a fact. The government system is not even close to adequate, not to mention that what they are learning is hostile to the Word of God (under the guise of "neutrality," remember), right down to the supposedly mundane facts. Government textbooks are written by people who are claiming to be neutral, when in reality, many textbook writers are unapologetically anti-Christian, secular humanists who hold to Marxist ideologies.

Secondly, people were successfully educated for centuries out of their homes and out of private, one-room schoolhouses. These methods cost nothing compared to what it costs to educate a child in any given public school. An article in *The Washington Post* entitled "The Real Cost of Public Schools" shocked people with this startling information:

> We're often told that public schools are underfunded. In the District [Washington, D. C.], the spending figure cited most commonly is $8,322 per child, but total spending is close to $25,000 per child.... [2]

What? If the government is actually spending close to $25,000 per child (which all comes out of our pockets) and only $8,000 of it goes toward the student, where is the other $17,000 of our money going? Not toward our kids' education. It's in the hands of greedy government bureaucrats and teachers unions. They take all that money from us for education, and it winds up providing the worst education in history and paying the government and unions an extraordinary amount to do it! In sharp contrast, the average cost per homeschool student is $546. Private schools also cost a great deal less and provide a much better education. The minute you privatize something, it creates a healthy competition. Competition is what drives prices down and quality up. This is a very good thing in the arena of education! When you lower the bar so that one size fits all—like government education has—you lower the quality and drive up the price. That is how the free market works versus government regulation.

The answer to educating our children without breaking God's Law is to get the government out of the business of education and privatize schools. God designed families and churches to educate—not the State. When the State steps in to do our job, God considers that an act of "tyranny."

Render Unto Whom?

The bottom line is that we have to understand nothing is free. Education is not free. Healthcare is not free. It is always paid by someone (the taxpayer), whether they want to or not. The government doesn't have any money—only people do. The government takes our money and then redistributes that money to wherever *it* decides it should go. It is playing the role of God.

God will not bless that act. Just because it has become legalized theft in our corrupt system does not make it okay with God. No matter how you slice it, the very root of the public school system breaks God's law of stealing and that should be a very serious crime to any Christian. The issue of taxes is a big topic. People love to quote "render unto Caesar what is Caesar's" without realizing the other part of that verse. "Render to Caesar the things that are Caesar's, and to God the things that are God's."

What does Caesar own? Caesar owns what it takes as its own, whether it breaks God's Laws or not. What does God own? The entire universe. We render to God what is God's: everything, including Caesar. "The earth is *Caesar's* and the fullness thereof." Oops, that's not quite right, is it? "The earth is the LORD's and the fullness thereof" (Ps. 24:1).

We must pay our taxes because we don't want to go to jail and because we must respect the authority over us. However, because "Caesar" claims something is his does not mean it is okay to break God's Law. It does not mean that as Christians, we do not work to change those ungodly laws with every breath that is in us. If Christians support and vote for a government that is breaking God's Law, we partake in the stealing of our neighbor's property too. It is a very dangerous thing when the church makes unholy alliances with the world. It brings upon itself disaster and judgment.

These are serious things to consider. We may not have all the alternative answers and solutions right off the top of our head, but the most important thing here is that we first realize where God draws the line: His commandments. When it comes to education, we must compare the system, its roots, its funding, its intentions, its results—and all other aspects—to the Word of God. That is what it means to be a real Christian.

2. *Whoever is not with me is against me, and whoever does not gather with me scatters.* (Matthew 12:30)

The verse above tells us there is no such thing as "neutrality." There is no gray area or middle ground. This applies especially when it comes to education. Most of us believe that the information we received from public schools and universities, the media, and the news is neutral. We believe they merely supply the facts and then those facts enter our neutral brains, at which point we come to our own objective conclusions. That is a lie from the pit of hell and the devil would love you to believe it. Don't forget that neutrality is a myth.

This is a fancy word, but we'll be using it a lot and it's an important word for you to remember. It is the word "presupposition." It simply refers to an underlying assumption or belief someone holds, whether or not they are conscious of holding it. When we tell our friend about how we somehow managed to fall off of a ladder, we have already *presupposed* or *assumed* the law of gravity. We don't question the law of gravity, or even attempt to explain it, because we have already assumed it is true. All information works this way. Webster's Dictionary says, "The existence of created things *presupposes* the existence of a Creator."[3]

Presuppositions are the basis for all worldviews. The atheist has very distinct assumptions about God (there isn't one), man (man is god), sin (there is no sin, only happiness and unhappiness), redemption (man can redeem himself) and eternity (there is no heaven or hell). All forms of religion and non-religion assume certain things that determine their beliefs.

So when it comes to our kids' education, the question isn't, "Is what they're getting biased?" The question is really, "*Whose* biases are they getting?" Is it the bias of the world and our civil government system? Or is it the bias of the Bible, which is infallible and inerrant? If God commands me to raise godly offspring, that means they need to start with biblical assumptions about the world concerning all information.

> 3. *A student is not above his teacher, but everyone who is fully trained will be like his teacher.* (Luke 6:40)

Who will be my child's teacher? Will it be someone with Caesar's stamp on them, who teaches in Caesar's courts, approved by Caesar? What if Caesar's teachers are Christian? Wouldn't that be the exception? Well maybe, but if Caesar's instructors teach anything from a biblical perspective, *they break the law.* The government forces teachers to teach from a humanist perspective commonly called "neutral." The government requires it by law.

What exactly is a humanist perspective? We covered this a little earlier, but humanism is a school of thought (just like New Age and other cults) that says God (or any religion) does not belong in education or any public place. Humanism is very much like atheism and the two go hand in hand. Here's a quick worldview comparison of humanism and Christianity:

Worldview:	Secular Humanism	Christianity
View of God	Atheism	Theism
View of Man	Product of Evolution	Product of Creation
View of Truth	Relative	Absolute
View of Knowledge	Experiential/Sensory	Divinely Revealed
View of Ethics	Situational	Universal

The government and the teachers unions control the content of the curriculum in which our children become discipled. They have a distinctly humanistic perspective. They write textbooks like this on purpose. No one formally teaches humanism out in the open, but after all the time the child spends learning from this perspective, it is all they know. This is why it's so dangerous. The schools are shaping both our kids' worldview and our culture without them even knowing it.

When our kids come home from school and we ask them, "What did you learn today?" what is the most common response? "Nothing." That is because *they don't know what they are learning*. They understand nothing about the underlying presuppositions they learn every day. Everything is normal to them. They don't have any other standard by which to compare what they're learning.

A *Really* Inconvenient Truth

The history of how our compulsory government education came about is extremely disturbing. If you ever do some research on your own, you will most likely find it very alarming and upsetting.[4] A couple things you need to know is that the current system we have adopted here in America originated 200 years ago in Prussia (today's East Germany). Its purpose was a means of indoctrinating a new generation of youth under a totalitarian leader. The entire grade-based, age-segregated school system came from the theory of evolution. In evolution, man was and is always evolving to different "stages." Men took the evolutionary model and decided to approach child training and education the same way. They got together and came up with a new system of schooling, and the first thing they did was make this form of indoctrination compulsory. This would get the children away from their parents' influence long enough for them to do their work. They also separated the children by age and subject. Traditionally, children would not split into "groups" and "grades." Subjects were usually taught as a whole, and not so distinctly.

The Idle Mind is Whose Playground?

This might be shocking to you, but there really was a strategy behind this method of new schooling. Eventually some American humanists took this model, adopted it, and designed an all-American version of this. These men were radical secular humanists. Their entire agenda for bringing government education about was to indoctrinate the whole country in humanism so they could bring about communism without a war. This is a fact. Their agenda has been extremely successful. They were up to no good and were not ashamed to say it. It is for this reason the church fought tooth and nail to oppose compulsory government education for over fifty years!

If you don't believe me, here it is, straight from the horse's mouth. Charles Potter was a signer of the *Humanist Manifesto* (their official "statement of faith," so to speak) and one of the architects of the public school system. He was unapologetic about their blatant intentions:

> Education is thus a most powerful ally of humanism, and every public school is a school of humanism. What can a theistic Sunday school, meeting for an hour once a week and teaching only a fraction of the children, do to stem the tide of a five-day program of humanistic teaching?[5]

This is the truth. This is the real system of philosophy and religion that is at the root of every textbook and teaching that kids at government schools receive. Don't be deceived: any philosophy that claims to be "non-religious" or "neutral" is actually very religious, in that it places man as god. Would you send your child to a Muslim school, where they would learn out of Muslim textbooks with Muslim-tainted versions of history, culture, math, science, music, and art, taught by Muslim teachers approved by Muslim officials? Would you send your child there for over 14,000 hours, for thirteen years, encourage them to have Muslim friends, and still expect them to graduate with a clear-thinking biblical worldview? Would you expect them be a Christian after one year? If your answer is no, then why would you send your child to an institution that is *just as religious and just as anti-Christian*?

4. *These commandments that I give you today are to be upon your hearts. Impress them on your children. Talk about them when you sit at home and when you walk along the road, when you lie down and when you get up.* (Deuteronomy 6:6–7)

The Bible says I, the parent, am to disciple my children from the moment they wake up to the moment they go to bed. How am I obeying this command when I willingly send them somewhere else for the majority of the day? And, even worse, if I send them to Caesar's court to be taught his standards, his view of reality and his worldview, is that submission and obedience to the Word of God? It is plain disobedience and rebellion.

Psalm 1 draws a clear line for us:

> *Blessed is the man*
> *who does not walk in the counsel of the wicked . . .*

How is this possible if our children are side by side with humanist children, learning humanist doctrine from wicked counselors?

> *. . . or stand in the way of sinners*
> *or sit in the seat of mockers . . .*

The entire content of government-written textbooks mocks God by implying in both subtle and blatant manners that God is not involved in science, math, social studies, physical education, art, or music. "Leave your beliefs at the door; you have now entered 'neutral' grounds." What a display of utter mockery.

> *. . . but his delight is in the law of the Lord,*
> *and on His Law he meditates day and night.*

The laws forbid children to bring Bibles to school; never mind delighting or meditating on it all day. The Bible tells us to pray without ceasing. Nope, can't do that either in that environment. We can't have the Ten Commandments anywhere on government property. We can't publicly declare His glory. This is a prison where Christianity is illegal. It is direct defiance; they have blown the war horn. Whose side are you on?

5. *Train a child in the way he should go, and when he is old he will not turn from it.* (Proverbs 22:6)

Who is training the mind of your child? Whoever does the teaching (which the Bible calls "discipling") steers and carves the path down which they will go. We think because we read our kids a picture-Bible, say grace at dinner, and take them to church, that qualifies as discipleship. Those things are good, but that is not real training. Let's look at the definition of training:

- To develop or form the habits, thoughts, or behavior of a child (or other person) by discipline and instruction.
- To make proficient by instruction and practice, as in some art, profession, or work to make (a person) fit by proper exercise, diet, practice, etc.

- To give the discipline and instruction, drill, practice, etc., designed to impart proficiency or efficiency.
- To get oneself into condition for an athletic performance through exercise, diet, practice.

The war we face in the years ahead for the survival of Christianity in our country is real. It is here. And we have been sending our children to the enemy's boot camp! If my kids are in government education, not only am I disobeying God's command to train my children in His ways, but I have also willingly given them over to the enemy. I have stared the opposition in the eye and said, "Absolutely. Go ahead. Drill my children. Instruct my children. Train them. Make them proficient and efficient in your system of thought and philosophy."

Evangelist Voddie Baucham said in a lecture, "If we continue to send our kids to Caesar for their education, we need to stop being surprised when they come home as Romans."

6. *Do not be yoked together with unbelievers. For what do righteousness and wickedness have in common? Or what fellowship can light have with darkness?* (2 Corinthians 6:14)

Why would I want my immature, sponge-brained children to be shaped and moulded by pagan, Caesar-worshiping children? I'd like to address the "salt 'n' light" argument for a minute. Just like the "render unto Caesar" argument, Christians often take Matthew 5:13–16 out of context and try to apply it to public school saying our kids are supposed to be salt and light in the world. Here is the scripture:

> *You are the salt of the earth. But if the salt loses its saltiness, how can it be made salty again? It is no longer good for anything, except to be thrown out and trampled by men. You are the light of the world. A city on a hill cannot be hidden. Neither do people light a lamp and put it under a bowl. Instead they put it on its stand, and it gives light to everyone in the house. In the same way, let your light shine before men, that they may see your good deeds and praise your Father in heaven.*

Jesus was speaking to His disciples. Keep in mind they were already grown adult believers and personal disciples of Jesus. Secondly, what is salt? It is a preservative. Preserving the earth is synonymous with taking dominion. The way to preserve and steward the earth is to train up Christian adults who understand man's calling, his responsibility and duty to redeem through the power of the Holy Spirit. They are to become godly thinkers and godly fighters.

Our children are not yet salt. Under the covenant God has made with us, we don't treat them as pagans, but instead, we train them in the way they should go. Their salvation is in God's hands.

But as parents, we must obey God in fulfilling what He has commanded of us. They will be a light one day, when they have reached spiritual maturity. They will be a light after their training is complete and they are equipped to do every good work. At that point, yes, they will be a light. Between birth to age eighteen, they are not mature or fully equipped yet. We don't know the state of their soul. Sure, there will be many evangelism opportunities in public school, but I must not be foolish—the world is evangelizing my child, not the other way around. Our children are swarmed every day with atheistic missionaries who desperately want my child to get "saved" from the religious bondage of Christ.

It is *because* we are to be salt and light and a city on a hill that we need to stay far away from Caesar's institution. We are to be distinct and different, set apart and holy.

I hope this chapter has sounded the alarm and has encouraged you to take this matter very seriously. May we all be challenged to search the Word for truth instead of "feeling out" this kind of history-changing decision. If you made it here without lighting a match to the pages, I am rejoicing! This is a really sensitive issue for us, but let's never put our own feelings ahead of God's feelings. That's the very bottom line, isn't it?

CHAPTER 9

Pabulum... Yum?

Jesus loves me, this I know... Most of us sang this song as kids if we grew up in church and then taught it to our own kids. It's a very sweet song... that does not convey the full gospel. While there is nothing wrong with singing sweet songs with the name "Jesus" in them, this shallow content has become the new standard of depth of the understanding of God—both in children and adults. I sing this song to my kids—don't get me wrong. But this song does not speak of sin, repentance, Christ's death, or resurrection. It just says, "Jesus loves me." That is not the *full gospel*. Know what I mean?

Shouldn't we have child-like faith? Yes, Jesus pointed out that unless we have the faith of a child, we cannot enter the Kingdom. Jesus did not say that we must have the *mind* of a child, or the *behavior* of a child. This simple faith requires that we believe what God says, and that is that. We enter the Kingdom with the faith of a child, but we don't stay there. Just as an infant is born and requires nothing more for food than simple milk, eventually that baby starts to grow and will need more nutrients. The baby's appetite increases and requires food that is more complex.

Eventually the child is able to eat steak and potatoes (maybe pureed at first). If you don't add nutrients and complex food into a child's diet, the child's health will suffer and he will experience growth problems. This is the same with our spiritual food. We begin with child-like faith, requiring only milk. Then we grow. We mature. As we gain more understanding, we require increasingly complex spiritual food. The Bible rebukes those of us who remain on spiritual baby food.

> *For though by this time you ought to be teachers, you need someone to teach you again the basic principles of the oracles of God. You need milk, not solid food, for everyone who lives on milk is unskilled in the word of righteousness, since he is a child.* (Hebrews 5:12–13)

The Bible equates living on spiritual milk with being unskilled in or unfamiliar with the Word. We lack understanding. I teach my children to memorize Scripture while they are children, but there will come a time when they must understand that which they have heard. They must know how to apply it in their lives and in the world. They will move on to real steak and potatoes and leave behind the pabulum they once ate as babies.

When pastors spoon-feed us baby pabulum from the pulpit Sunday after Sunday, maybe for fear of offending people, all it does is breed ignorance and invite God's rebuke. God is harsh because of the level of impact this ignorance has on the community and culture around us. These days, we constantly hear popular self-help what-can-Jesus-do-for-*me* messages about how Jesus is our non-judgmental friend and God is not the angry God of the Old Testament anymore. This gives people and communities wrong ideas, and results in them not being properly equipped with answers and directives for life.

With this kind of prevailing message, people do not know that God has specific blueprints for things like child training, education, how we should vote, how we should take care of the poor (including single moms and aging parents), answers for bad economies, and all the family and moral issues we face today.

As a result (and this is the scary part), the church doesn't look any different from the world. We vote the same way. We marry and divorce the same way (and research shows it might be worse in the church). We spend our leisure time the same way. We send our kids to the same schools. We behave and talk the same way with some added Christian jargon. We think about social issues the same way. We are indistinguishable from the godless culture of our time!

What should God do with us? We deserve nothing but judgment. We are supposed to be a city on a hill that cannot be hidden. We are supposed to be so different and so bright that no one can miss it from miles away.

We Are Big Babies

Do not be conformed to this world, but be transformed by the renewal of your mind, that by testing you may discern what is the will of God, what is good and acceptable and perfect. (Romans 12:2)

We have conformed to the world. We have given our minds over to worldly cultural influence because we are no longer able to discern what is good and acceptable and perfect according to God. Just look at the corruption within the church right now: we have prevailing homosexuality within the church and within the leadership of the church. We have gender role confusion in the home and in church leadership. We have divorce rates that put to shame the name of Christ.

Between seventy and eighty-five percent of our children leave the faith by the time they finish high school—and some studies show this is actually the case by the time they reach middle school! We have Christians promoting the kind of government that God hates—the kind that tries to control and regulate our lives. This is a crisis.

You see, what is going on in the world is a reflection of what has been going on in the church for a long while. If we don't like what is going on in the world, we need to fix the church first. Get off the milk and return to solid food. "But solid food is for the mature, for those who have their powers of discernment trained by constant practice to distinguish good from evil" (Heb. 5:14).

We need to mature. We need to understand far more than "Jesus loves me, this I know." We need training and constant practice on how to distinguish right from wrong. Many within these lukewarm environments are unable to tell the difference. Until we start getting meat and potatoes from the pulpit and are equipped in discernment in "the basic principles" of God, we will continue to see a decline inside and outside the church. Not a very nice thought, when you consider that our kids and grandkids will have to live in that world.

The good news is that housewives can do something about this! We can change the course of this path right now! Let me show you how.

A THREE COURSE MEAL

1. To change the world, housewives will need a sound *theology*.

What is theology? And why should you care? Theology is the system of beliefs you hold about God. All other beliefs rest upon this foundation. Your presuppositions—or underlying assumptions about the world—determine what kind of theology you have. The kind of teaching you've had about God from Sunday school teachers, your parents, the secular culture, and your pastor also shape your theology. When we think about how we affect our little corner of our world, it is critical that we take a close look at the theology we hold. We need to make sure it is on target. We looked at the basic questions within a worldview earlier. Let's quickly go over the answers. These are not formal answers, but they are orthodox answers put in my own words.

> **View of God**: Is there one? Many? What is He like: personal or impersonal?
>
> *Answer*: There is only one God. He exists in three persons: Father, Son and Holy Spirit. He is personal.

View of Man: Where did we come from? Why are we here? Is man God?

Answer: Man was created by God, which is part of His whole creation. Man is fallen and sinful. Man cannot help or redeem himself. Only the grace of God can redeem him. Man's main purpose is to glorify God and to enjoy Him forever.

View of Knowledge: How do we know things? Is the material world and our five senses the be-all and end-all?

Answer: God has revealed knowledge to us through general revelation and through special revelation: the Holy Scriptures.

View of Ethics: Is there a standard of ethics (right and wrong) for every nation and culture, or does it depend upon what each individual culture agrees is right?

Answer: God is the standard and measure of all truth. We determine truth and ethical standards by comparing everything to His Word. God's truth is universal and absolute. There is no such thing as "situational ethics."

The Barna Research group has also asked people these questions to determine if they have a biblical worldview. They discovered a very alarming fact: only 9% of born-again Christians have a biblical worldview! And only half of pastors have a biblical worldview! That is so staggering! Is it any wonder why things are in such rough shape? Ask yourself these same questions and let's see how you do:

1. Is there absolute moral truth?
2. Is the Bible infallible and without error?
3. Is Satan a real being?
4. Did Jesus live a sinless life when He was on earth?
5. Is God the all-powerful, all-knowing Creator of the Universe who still rules over it today?
6. Is it possible to go to heaven for being a "good person?"

Answers:

1. Yes. God is the standard for all truth. Truth is not situational. God is "the Way, the Truth, and the Life."

2. Yes. The Word of God is perfect. (We are not talking about typos, we are talking about content.)

3. Yes. He is a created being—a fallen angel that rebelled against God. He is at work to deceive the world so they will be damned along with him.

4. Yes. Jesus is God incarnate. He was fully human and fully God. Because of this, He was tempted, but never once sinned.

5. Yes. God is sovereign. God sees all things and can do all things. He is the Creator and Ruler. Jesus is ruling and reigning today from His throne in heaven.

6. No. No one can earn salvation by good deeds or behavior. No person can save himself. Only when God bestows His grace on someone will that person be born again and repent of their sins. Salvation is by grace alone.

How did you do? If your answers looked very different, you may be surprised and alarmed. That's okay. The idea is for all of us to recognize how far off the beaten track we are—so we can get on course and continue!

The first thing we need to do in order to change the world is to change our thinking. Make sure it really lines up with the Bible. We can't give our children what we don't have. We must start with a solid foundation, which is solid biblical doctrine. Remember, the Bible is clear about how important this is:

> *If anyone teaches a different doctrine and does not agree with the sound words of our Lord Jesus Christ and the teaching that accords with godliness, he is puffed up with conceit and understands nothing.* (1 Timothy 6:3–4)

Lack of understanding is to God the same as conceit or arrogance. It's as if we are saying we're too good for knowledge, or whatever excuse we have. Also, keep this in mind: we are always living out our theology and teaching it to our children, even unconsciously. Even when we claim we don't know what our theology is, we already have one. The choices we make and the words we speak to our husbands and children are all stemming from this theology.

It is dangerous when we are not aware of the theology we really hold. If our theology contains errors in some areas, we are unknowingly teaching our kids and those around us those errors as well. That will continue through generations. Can you imagine—a whole line of true Christianity broken, all because we women didn't have our theology in check? It is imperative we get this right, because slight deviations from God's Word lead to pseudo-Christian cults.

This happened with the Mormons. A man named Joseph Smith just changed a little thing here and a little thing there. Before long, he was leading an entirely different religion. And the confusing thing is that he used all the same terminology as orthodox Christianity, which led many well-meaning Christians down the wrong path. The Mormons claim to believe in Jesus, the Son of God, the Trinity, the cross, and many other Christian concepts. But if we look below the surface, we realize we are saying the same words, but they mean different things. The Mormon Jesus is the brother of Satan. The Mormon Jesus is a created being—in fact, he was originally a man who became a god. The Mormon version of Jesus says He came to be by means of God having physical relations with Mary. The Mormon "Trinity" is not a triune Godhead, as orthodox Christians believe; they are three separate and distinct gods. They are three of many, maybe thousands, or millions of other gods in the universe. They are what you call "polytheists," *poly* meaning "many" and *theists* meaning "gods."

As you can see, little deviations can lead to devastating spiritual consequences. If we don't have the right Jesus, we don't have salvation. It becomes "another gospel" and that gospel does not save. This is why we must make sure that every belief we have, every understanding we have of God, and everything we confess is true and accurate. We know how many Mormons there are in the world today—fourteen million—all because one man perpetuated his theological errors. It is high time that wives and moms wise up, get a grip, and get a hold of their theology.

2. **Revolutionary women need to learn basic *apologetics*.**

> *We demolish arguments and every pretension that sets itself up against the knowledge of God, and we take captive every thought to make it obedient to Christ. And we will be ready to punish every act of disobedience, once your obedience is complete.* (2 Corinthians 10:5–6)

The word apologetics does not mean we "apologize" for something. It means to make a reasoned defense of something or someone. In Christianity, it simply means to know what you believe (theology) and why you believe it (apologetics).

The Bible tells us we must demolish arguments that set themselves against the knowledge of God. *Demolish*. This means we need to know and understand what we're talking about. Every Christian should be able to defend the gospel to anyone who challenges or asks.

There are millions of us Christians walking around, and it would seem to the rest of the world that we're pretty dumb. I don't mean to insult anyone, but we are so often blown away by any worldly intelligent answer, we just shrug it off and say, "Oh well, I just have child-like faith." Friends, this is not a witness for Christ. Christians are supposed to be the wisest people on the earth! No longer will we surrender our minds to mediocrity. If we are going to change the world as Christ commanded, it's time to smarten up! You might ask, "Is this really necessary?" Well, what does the Word of God say? "Always be prepared to give an answer to everyone who asks you to give the reason for the hope that you have. But do this with gentleness and respect" (1 Pet. 3:15).

We are to demolish false arguments and always be prepared. That means we have to have studied what we believe and why we believe it ahead of time. It also means we know a little about the strategies and arguments the enemy is using to deceive the world. This involves a bit of effort. We don't have to know everything, but there are simple answers that do what they are intended to do: give an answer, tell of the hope we have, and expose the unbeliever's foolishness according to God. We do this respectfully and gently, but we must do it nonetheless.

Some of us may have witnessed Christians who have tried to defend the faith and wound up embarrassing the faith instead. Maybe they became angry and rude. Some of us have also witnessed brothers and sisters who have been enticed into a debate where the unbeliever's objective was to get the Christian to sin by making them angry. They set out to mock them, and the Christian fell for it. This is called a "tar-baby." The intention was to lure them in so they could fall into the trap. It happens all the time. We are to watch out for this kind of enemy strategy. We have to be on our guard. I believe that situation is preventable if we are really prepared as the Bible commands us to be. We must be wise to the intent of the unbeliever. We need to first discern why they are engaging in discussion with us. Are they really interested to know? Are they really looking for answers and struggling to find them? Or can you detect that they want to corner you and mock the faith? Some of this discernment comes with practice and maturity. We need to seek both of those things.

An apologist named Greg L. Bahnsen once said in a lecture, "Our job as Christians is to shut the mouths of the unbelievers. It is the Lord's job to open their hearts." We must keep that in mind when we come into discussions with people online or in person. We are not the Holy Spirit; we cannot convict anyone's heart. However, the Bible instructs us to speak the truth in love. You never know how God will use your conversation to plant a seed or convict them of their sin later on. It is simply a part of fulfilling the Great Commission: discipling the nations. It's declaring God's sovereignty over every part of this world, including the unbelieving parts.

How wonderful it would be to see churches offering classes in apologetics for the congregations. This could make a huge impact in your local community. You could first learn about methods of defending the faith, and effective ways to do so. Then, learn about the predominant non-Christian religions in your community. In my community, it would be Sikhism, Mormonism, Jehovah's Witnesses, and atheism. Don't forget—atheism is just as much a religion as anything else. We could learn about the basic tenets of these faiths. We could learn how to show others the way they collapse in the light of the Word. This could prepare you for the next time you get that knock on your door, or when you're standing in line somewhere… If only we would be prepared!

Don't Forget the Little Ones

Another potent way of really make an impact on the whole world is teaching our children apologetics. Imagine your seven-, eight- or nine-year-old able to articulate why you have to believe in God in order for anything in the world to make sense, including your own name. This is actually a complex idea but can be explained simply enough to kids. Here's an example:

"Atheists are people who don't believe in God. They say that unless we can touch something with our hands or observe it, it doesn't exist. I guess they can't believe in their own name, can they? They can't pull their name out of the refrigerator, can they? But what if they write their name on a piece of paper? Does it exist now? Well maybe, but if we light that piece of paper on fire and throw it away, does that mean they don't have a name anymore? Of course not. Their name is not 'material.' We can't actually see, feel, taste or touch someone's name. Their name is what we call an 'idea' or 'concept.' God is not material either. We can't pull God out of the refrigerator. But God exists, just like your name."

Imagine having a child who can understand and articulate something like this. These kids are out there, right now. A new generation of parents has emerged—parents who teach their kids how to think! These kids understand why a Biblical worldview makes more sense than any other worldview out there. These kids are going to grow up and become world leaders that are submissive to the Lordship of Christ! Teaching a child to think in this way will alter the course of history. We will be setting them on a path that will affect who they marry, what they do in this world, how many children they have, and how far and vast they take dominion for the glory of God. That legacy will continue down the generational line. Attention moms: we have a responsibility to set them on this course!

3. **History-maker moms need to understand *evangelism*.**

Evangelism starts in the home. This is the primary task and focus of raising children. We are teaching them the ways of God and their need for salvation. If your husband isn't a Christian, you are setting an example, praying for him and leading him to the Lord through your actions. Evangelism is the first step to discipleship, though it does not end there. Notice what Jesus commands in the Great Commission:

> *And Jesus came and said to them, "All authority in heaven and on earth has been given to me. Go therefore and make disciples of all nations, baptizing them in the name of the Father and of the Son and of the Holy Spirit, teaching them to observe all that I have commanded you."*
> (Matthew 28:18–20)

It is obvious that making disciples first involves teaching them about God: they must understand sin and their need to repent. But it goes far beyond that. We are to baptize them and teach them the commandments, which is God's Law/Word, His morality and His system of thought. This is how the Kingdom of God expands: when individuals repent and believe, their hearts are changed. They are now receptive to God's plan. This begins to affect their families, which in turn affects the whole culture. Studies show that when a man comes to church, his whole family follows. When a man leaves the church, the same thing happens. Right now, we have churches full of women and not nearly as many men. In one video interview, Mark Driscoll of Mars Hill Church elaborated on this point:

> You walk in… and it's sea-foam green, and fuchsia and lemon yellow. The whole architecture and the whole aesthetic is real feminine. The preacher is kind of feminine, and the music is emotional and feminine. We're looking around going, "How come we're not innovative?" Because all the innovative dudes are at home watching football. Or they're off making money, or climbing a mountain, or shooting a gun, or working on their truck. They're going to get married, make money, have babies, build companies, and buy real estate. They are going to make the culture of the future. If you get the young men, you win the war. You get everything: the families, the women, the children, the money, the business… you get everything. If you don't get the young men, you get nothing.[1]

Churches need to look at these facts and refocus their efforts to evangelize and disciple the young men of the community. Secondly, those of us who have sons need to pay attention to this. Our sons will make the culture. We need to keep tight reigns on these boys and see to it that we do not neglect their evangelism and discipleship. Our boys will win the culture wars (and, of course, our girls who will eventually raise more boys). Keep these things in mind at all times.

We also need to learn how to present the gospel once again. I cannot remember the last time I heard of a congregation being trained in how to present the gospel to strangers, and then going out and doing it. It used to be more popular in years past, during the "fire and brimstone" days. Many people within the church did not like it. Some people were converted, but were not discipled, and ended up more bitter towards Christianity than they were before their conversion. There were many pros and cons to those days, but one thing is for sure: street preaching happened a lot more often. We do have other means of declaring the gospel in addition to street ministries, like Internet blogs and media, etc. But we mustn't neglect the personal, face-to-face approach of articulating and presenting the gospel. I write to myself here too. I cannot remember the last time I walked up to someone, started a conversation, and asked them if they knew they were a sinner or if they had asked God for forgiveness. When is the last time I told someone about the cross? Why are we not being encouraged or equipped to do this anymore? It seems intimidating at first, doesn't it? The thought of randomly talking to a stranger and bringing up Jesus and sin doesn't sound appealing. But doing this is not a suggestion. God commands it of us. I think the more we obey, the easier it gets, just like anything else.

From time to time, I enjoy listening to Wretched Radio on Sirius Radio, a Christian radio program that includes Christian news… and a lot of sarcasm and satire. But I really enjoy when they have "Witness Wednesdays." I can't tell you how much I've learned from hearing live conversations of Todd presenting the gospel to people. While live on the air, Todd will be on a college campus, or somewhere heavily populated. He walks up to someone with his microphone and asks if he can ask him or her some questions.

He usually starts out by asking them what they're doing, or what they're wearing if he notices an interesting t-shirt or piece of jewelry, or perhaps what they are studying. Within a couple minutes, they are already onto religion. He begins to find out what they believe. Sometimes they know. Sometimes they don't know. Sometimes their beliefs are so confused it's as if they hit a religion buffet and just piled a bunch of stuff on their plate.

Todd is prepared for the most common answers and reactions. Nothing takes Todd by surprise, or if it does, he does not seem thrown by it. He never gets offended and always uses humor if he can, to keep things light, but not too light. He gets to their underlying presupposition and reveals it to them.

He always brings up what they believe and then compares it to the Ten Commandments. One conversation went like this:

"Are you familiar with the Bible?"

"A little bit."

"The Bible says this: It is appointed unto man that you will die one time, and then get judged. So chances are you're going to eventually die just like the rest of us, right?" (The young man is agreeing and nodding.) "I'm going to give you an examination to see what might happen to you when you die, alright?" He agrees. "I'm going to do that by holding up the Ten Commandments. Have you ever heard of those?"

"Yes."

"Okay. Do you know any of them?"

"Um… Yes."

"Alright. For instance, the Bible says—one of the Commandments says—'Thou shalt not lie'. Have you ever done that?"

"Yes."

"So if I tell a lie, what would you call me? What type of person am I?"

"A liar."

"Okay, so would you agree that you are a liar?"

"Hmm…"

"Well you just called me a liar; that was pretty easy. Have you ever stolen anything?"

"Yes."

"What does that make you?"

"A thief."

"This one gets a little tougher. Are you ready? Jesus—have you heard of Him? Yes, okay. So Jesus said, "You've heard it said 'Thou shalt not commit adultery'—one of the commandments—'But I say that if you look at a woman with lust, you've committed adultery in your heart.' Have you ever done that?"

"Yeah."

"Okay, so by your own admission: a liar, a thief, an adulterer at heart. You have to face God and He gives you the same examination. Do you think He'd find you innocent or guilty?"

"God would probably find me innocent—*if* I ask for forgiveness."

> "Well, that's interesting, because if you stood before a judge and you had broken the laws and you asked for forgiveness, would the judge say 'Oh, you're sorry. Okay, I'll let you go?'"
>
> "Well, if it's the same standard, then yeah, I would be a liar and a thief, etc. God would find me guilty."
>
> "Now it gets a little harder. If you're guilty of breaking the Laws, and God is a just Judge, and must punish criminals, would He send you to heaven or to hell?"
>
> "He would send me to hell."
>
> "Right. So what do you know about hell?"
>
> "It's a place where you are punished for eternity. A horrible place."
>
> "So if God exists, and if He judges you, and if the standard is the Ten Commandments, you'd be going to hell? Does that kind of make you go 'Yikes!'?"
>
> "A little bit, yes."

The conversation continued and the young man expressed that he hoped God wouldn't judge him in the same way He judged a murderer or someone who has committed greater crimes. Todd humbly helped him to see that while God is loving and kind, He is also just. He doesn't want to send people to hell, because the reality is that if He sent everyone to Hell who broke His Laws, everyone would be going to hell. We have all broken the commandments. Not one single person has kept them. So since God is a just God and can't let people break His Laws, He has a plan that demonstrates both His lovingkindness and His justice. Todd told him then about how Jesus died on the cross on our behalf for the laws we have broken. He presented the full gospel. He gave him the bad news and then the good news. Near the end, Todd asked the young man, to make sure he understood the gospel:

> "So tell me, in your own words, what are the two things you must do to be saved?"
>
> The young man replied, "I have to repent, and place my trust in the hands of Jesus."

In this situation, Todd encountered a receptive person who was humble and honest in his answers. This is not always the case. This is why it is good to be a little prepared for different encounters. Many training sources are available for help with this.

Here are a few general witnessing tips from Todd:

1. Start in the natural. This means start the conversation about something non-spiritual.

2. Swing to the supernatural. After you've established some common ground and relationship, move the conversation to the spiritual side of things.

3. Open God's Law. This is where we do the examination. Use as many of the Ten Commandments as you can.

4. Warn of God's judgment. After it is revealed that they have broken God's Law, this is a good place to say that the Bible speaks of heaven and hell. You can say, "If God judged you based on how you did with these commandments, and He is a just and righteous God, what should He do with you? What do you deserve?" Even if they refuse to acknowledge with their mouths at this point, their spirit knows they deserve God's judgment.

5. Present law to the proud; grace to the humble. If the sinner is proud and self-righteous, uphold the Law. If the sinner is broken-hearted and contrite, offer grace.

6. Share the good news!

7. Call them to repentance and faith.[2]

In summary, when wives and moms get a grip on their presuppositions, their theology, their apologetics, and evangelism, there is victory on the horizon! God promises us. We are on our way to making significant change in our own lives and on the whole world. This is the proper proclaiming of the Gospel starting with proclaiming it to our children and our community. After that, the world will transform in great multitudes. This is what Jesus meant when He said we would do greater things than even He did. Jesus performed amazing miracles and converted dozens and hundreds. Now we have the outpouring of the Holy Spirit through the preaching of the Word. Now entire nations will bow their knees! Just obey, be faithful to this calling, and then watch!

CHAPTER 10

Politics, Schmolitics

We need to accept problems and testing as a condition of life. Even in Eden, apart from the problems of farming, Adam and Eve were every day put to the test. The tree of the knowledge of good and evil could be bypassed or not. God presented them always with the problem of faith and obedience.[1]

 am like many Christian stay-at-home moms: it is very easy for me to lose sight of anything going on in the world outside my own four walls. We get caught up in our own problems and cares.

Sometimes it's as though nothing exists outside the squabbles we dealt with today, or the food we cleaned off the floor, or the to-do list we never got to do.

We have our own lives, our marriages to deal with, our in-laws, our friends, our birthday parties, our bills, and our shopping lists. What else is there to worry about besides that? Why would we burden ourselves with all the drama of the news or the political climate in the world? We have enough on our shoulders, don't we? We have enough pressure and stress to deal with as it is, right? We think to ourselves that someone else will deal with that stuff. We'll leave that realm to "the experts" or other, better-educated Christians. We think that we cannot really make a difference in this world, especially when it comes to the big issues like laws the government passes, and taxes, and that kind of thing. We just mind our own business and worry about our own problems.

While this is by far the easiest road to take, I'd like to test this mentality. Shall we compare this attitude with the Bible and see if it lines up? Let's see if it passes the test. Let's see what happens long term when we think this way.

If you live in an area that experiences frequent storms and hurricanes, I'm sure you would agree most people are very prepared for it. They have emergency medical kits, flashlights, extra food, and water on hand in the basement. They get special storm windows, radios, and batteries. They are prepared for whatever may come, and they have thought ahead and acted on it. If they don't, they put their whole family in danger.

This is how Christians should think about the world. The enemy has many insidious plans to try to thwart God's plans and authority. It has always been this way—since Eden. If you look throughout history, there were seasons where it appeared the enemy was winning. But we are a very short-sighted people. We do not look at history as a whole. We tend to get caught up in our own moment in time. We see the here and now, and nothing more. We come to our conclusions about God and His hand on history based on this *now* experience.

We must remember that there are two orders in this world: God's world order and Satan's fake world order, which we call "the world system." A constant clash and battle occurs throughout history between these world systems. We already know who *has* won, *is* winning, and will *continue* to win. Satan already knows this, and cannot stand it and will continue to drag anyone down that he can. God has a plan for science and technology; economics and medicine; art and all education.

God has His Kingdom here on earth, and yes—the kingdom is here now (Jesus established it as His birth, death, resurrection, and ascension)—and for every plan and order God has, Satan has set up a counterfeit. Satan has a counterfeit kingdom. He has a counterfeit gospel that comes under all false religions, including atheism and secular humanism. He has a counterfeit order.

But understand this important thing: Satan is only "the god of this world" in the sense that he is the god over his own counterfeit system. He is not the literal God of the cosmos. He does not rule and reign. He has no sovereignty, no power or dominion here. Satan has always been on a leash. The leash was a little longer before the cross. After the cross, that leash got tight.

This is why we must acknowledge man is inherently evil. If we take Satan right out of the picture, we will still commit atrocities and do the most wretched and terrible things. Without Satan within 100 miles, we are still disgusting in our sin. We still reject the Savior. We still will not obey. We still try to usurp His rightful authority over our lives and the world.

I think Satan gets a lot of credit for stuff he doesn't do. Having said that, I believe he is a real force in the world. I believe he does still have influence. He has rebelled and will try to convince the world to rebel along with him until God throws him in the pit at the Last Day.

The bright hope we have, though, is that things will not always look like they are getting worse. It looks this way right now. That is because we are in the middle of a historical cycle of rebellion, judgment, and then revival. Just read through Christian history and you will see this cycle occur repeatedly. I will show you why doom is not our destiny. I mean that for here on this earth, in the physical and material.

God doesn't have any problems in heaven. He's not concerned with what's going on up there. All the problems are here on this earth, which is why Jesus prayed, "Your will be done on earth, as it is [already] in Heaven," and why He declared, "All authority has been given to me in Heaven and earth."

The old song that goes, "This earth is not my home; I'm just a-passing through," actually proposes an anti-Christian idea. God gave us a mandate in Genesis to care for and govern the created order. He told us to multiply and fill the earth. Then He told us in the New Testament to go and make disciples of all nations. The Bible says the earth is our home. Until the Lord's second return, this is where our work is. This is where we are to plant our roots and feet firmly. We are not to have the attitude of *Jesus is coming back any minute now, so don't worry about the state of the world.*

God expects us to be problem solvers! We are not to ask God to take us out of here so we don't have to deal with it. As Dennis Peacock joked in a lecture, "God is not up in heaven saying, 'Oh, my little darling children, I just can't wait to take you home!' No, He's probably saying something like, 'When will my idiot kids wake up, so they can finally do the work I have for them?'"

We have a lot of work to do. We have a big mess to clean up that the previous generation didn't want to clean up. They gave up their dominion because they thought the end was near and the Rapture was going to happen in their lifetime. Now we are living in a "post-Christian" world because of that forfeit.

The good news is that things don't have to continue like this if we get to work. We need to concern ourselves with what is going on in the world, what the enemy's plans are, and how we're going to prepare for it as well as fight it.

In what kind of world do you want your child to grow up? What about your grandchildren? If we don't do something now, the enemy is happy to take care of things for us. Let's look at how strongly Jesus felt about this:

> *Hypocrites! You know how to discern the face of the sky, but you cannot discern the signs of the times.* (Matthew 16:3)

Jesus blatantly rebuked the Pharisees and Sadducees for understanding and predicting petty things like the weather, yet they were oblivious to the wickedness in their culture. They were ignorant of what God truly required of them. I think that sometimes we are guilty of this too as wives and moms. We expect other people to think about the hard stuff and give ourselves permission to be ignorant.

Here are a few excuses I have used in the past. Perhaps you can relate.

1. "Understanding the times and the realm of politics should be left to men."

   You are the salt of the earth. But if the salt loses its saltiness, how can it be made salty again? It is no longer good for anything, except to be thrown out and trampled by men. (Matthew 5:13)

Yes, men must understand the times and be involved, but women are not exempt from this. Jesus said we are the salt of the earth. That includes women. Salt wasn't just to "add flavor" to a bland world. We talked previously about how salt was a preservative. Christians are to preserve the earth by upholding the Law, obeying God's commands and fulfilling the Great Commission. Jesus said, "If the salt loses its saltiness, how can it be made salty again? It is no longer good for anything, except to be thrown out and trampled by men." If we look at history, every time the church disengages, pulls back, refuses to get their hands dirty and becomes irrelevant in the culture, the forces of evil and humanism rise to the challenge. What follows is usually the horrid persecution of the church. The scary and sobering part is that the Bible agrees that if we, the preservatives, are useless, the only thing we are good for is trampling. Ladies, it's time to get involved. No more excuses!

2. "We're not called to politics; we're only called to preach the Gospel."

   I tell you the truth, until heaven and earth disappear, not the smallest letter, not the least stroke of a pen, will by any means disappear from the Law until everything is accomplished. (Matthew 5:18)

Christ declared that the Kingdom was *at hand*, meaning *any time now*. Through His death, resurrection and ascension, Christ established the Kingdom on earth, all authority was given to Him, and Satan was eternally defeated. Christ now sits at the Father's right hand and rules from His throne. He will reign there "till His enemies are made His footstool" (Heb. 10:12).

The second accomplishment is the progressive and total fulfillment of the Great Commission. Jesus declared that it *will* be accomplished. God has promised us victory. Until heaven and earth disappear, the Law is the standard by which we disciple the nations. Sinners don't know they are sinners until they first see that they have fallen short of something. Discipling begins with showing the nations God's Law; it is the beginning of evangelism. The second part to evangelism is showing them the grace Jesus offers if they repent and believe. People must first understand why God is saving them and why they are repenting.

God's Law also serves as the foundation for running all societies. In the spiritual, it reveals sin; it rewards obedience and points to Christ. In the practical, it punishes law-breakers, protects law-keepers, and points to Christ. God's Law is beneficial to all societies, even unbelievers! This is not the only purpose of the Great Commission. God has a plan of redemption for this earth. His plan is to restore all the earth to His original pre-curse condition. We will get into that exciting bit a little later. God isn't just concerned with our spiritual health, He means to redeem and restore all spheres and facets of life: and that includes everything from pizza delivery to politics to nuclear physics. Nothing will remain unredeemed in God's plan. This means we must strive to steward every aspect of life, and this includes the political realm. I know I get overwhelmed when I look at what it takes to change laws, but you'd be surprised at how much of a difference one person can make. One letter, one news story, one passionate person can cause a total stir in the media and culture. This has happened both for better and worse repeatedly. Leaving politics to the system of the world, which is anti-Christian, is not wise at all. Now is the time to act and bring God's standards into this arena.

3. "We're supposed to obey those in authority over us, unless it directly opposes God."

Anyone who breaks one of the least of these commandments and teaches others to do the same will be called least in the kingdom of heaven, but whoever practices and teaches these commands will be called great in the kingdom of heaven. (Matthew 5:19)

I find that it's easy for us to make the mistake of believing a national rebellion hasn't taken place unless Christianity is actually outlawed. We should keep in mind that anytime God's Law is broken, those lawbreakers oppose God. Anytime the government passes a law that breaks a commandment in one form or another, it has opposed God and called it "legal" and "official." Do you think God overlooks this?

Consider just one of the Ten Commandments—stealing. We looked at this before. What is socialism? Very simply, it is taking money from citizens by force, and then redistributing it as the government sees fit. It seeks to rob from the better-off and "donate" to the less better-off. What part of this *isn't* stealing? Even were it for a good cause, God still sees it as breaking His Law. He will not bless a nation that legislates the breaking of His Law. Jesus said, "Thy kingdom come on earth as it is in heaven." Do you think the issue of killing babies or homosexuality is a touchy subject in heaven? No! God's problems are not in heaven. Whatever is God's will in heaven, it is also His will here on earth.

4. "The Bible says we're supposed to *render unto Caesar what is Caesar's*."

   The earth is the Lord's, and everything in it. The world and all its people belong to Him. (Psalm 24:1)

We looked at this earlier also, as one of the most over-quoted verses in the Bible and one of the most misunderstood. First, we don't answer to Caesar, we answer to God—and Caesar answers to God, whether Caesar will admit it or not. Here is an important point: just because something "belongs" to Caesar doesn't mean it is not violating God's Law and that we shouldn't work to change it. God requires us to!

When our laws oppose God's Law, we oppose God Himself. Do we think that because our disobedience is "legal" God will overlook our crime? No. He will punish the law-breakers. He will disinherit them.

The scripture above rebukes believers who break the commandments and teach others to do the same. Do you support a government that believes in socialism? More importantly, are you working with your family and community to reverse the laws that transgress God's commands? If not, we are sentencing our children to a world of corruption and judgment.

5. "Politics just isn't my thing."

   For it pleased the Father that in Him all the fullness should dwell, and by Him to reconcile all things to Himself, by Him, whether things on earth or things in heaven.... (Colossians 1:19–20)

Politics may not be your thing, but understanding the times and responding to them biblically *is* your thing. God requires it of every Christian. We mustn't say "this isn't my thing" as though working together to keep God's Law is optional; as though it's a matter of preference, or something you get to pick, like what shirt you're going to wear. Politics is the business of every Christian because it is our duty to uphold God's standards in every arena of life. We are responsible to God for who we elect. Here's something to think about. If the majority of people elect corrupt politicians, it is because we did not disciple the nation. Every Christian contributes either actively or passively. We are actively making a difference if we get involved, take action and disciple our community in the ways of the Lord. We are passively contributing if we do not get involved, which allows secular authorities to step in and have their way. In either case, both actions are contributing to the discipling of our country... or sentencing it to judgment.

As wives and mothers, our goal is to leave our children an inheritance they can pass down through generations: a godly legacy. We pray that they will live in a godlier, more prosperous country. If you look at your actions right now, if you look at how you discern and respond to the times, which inheritance are you contributing to—an inheritance of blessing and promise? Or an inheritance full of the wrath and judgment of God?

6. "It's too big a task."

> *We demolish arguments and every pretension that sets itself up against the knowledge of God, and we take captive every thought to make it obedient to Christ. And we will be ready to punish every act of disobedience, once your obedience is complete.* (2 Corinthians 10:5–6)

It really can seem overwhelming at times. It seems like Christianity is dying out and Islam and other anti-Christian institutions are winning. We have to keep in mind that things happen in cycles. There are times of rebellion, spiritual growth, persecution, and revival. I don't think this cycle is always inevitable, but it seems God's people keep forgetting about what is so important to the Lord: upholding His righteousness in every sphere of life. When we make unholy alliances with the government; we give our children to them to disciple; we hand over our Christian duties a little bit here, a little bit there, and fifty years later, you can't even tell we are Christians... well do we deserve persecution? We have forsaken our calling! We have become total wimps in society and traded godliness and holiness for political correctness.

And friends, the longer we wait to change things, the bigger the task it will become! But even worse, we will be heaping that burden on our children's children. We want to put an end to rebellion now. We want to stand up to the enemy and his system and say, "This is not your domain! You have no right to rule here. The earth is the Lord's and the fullness thereof! We are taking back what rightfully belongs to Him!" We must not say this with just words, but with deeds.

Take your children out of the hands of the enemy: get them out of the public schools! Let's stop relying on Veggie Tales and an hour at Sunday school to train and disciple our children! Let's actively commit to teaching our own children. Let's do what we can in our own community. Let's find a biblical solution to poverty that will actually help people come out of poverty, not just give them handouts that cripple them in the long run. Let's work to change unbiblical laws. All this can realistically happen. Jesus promised that we are not alone. Obedience requires sacrifice, but the rewards are generational. Victory is ours, as promised.

We must first understand the arguments and pretensions that are setting themselves up against the knowledge of God. This includes every humanist institution, especially government schools. If every Christian parent were to take their children out of government schools, and had them in private or home schools, that would send a message loud and clear!

It's time to pull out God's weapon of mass reconstruction: the family. When families fulfill the dominion mandate to steward the earth, multiply, and teach their children to obey the commands, nothing can stop them. In the long-term, they are invincible because they are in the will of God. If every church encouraged these actions, discipling the nations would not be so great a task. In fact, I believe it would be attainable within one or two generations!

7. "The Bible says women shouldn't be in authority."

> *Then Mordecai told them to return this answer to Esther, "Do not flatter yourself that you shall escape in the king's palace any more than all the other Jews. For if you keep silent at this time, relief and deliverance shall arise for the Jews from elsewhere, but you and your father's house will perish. And who knows but that you have come to the kingdom for such a time as this and for this very occasion?"* (Esther 4:13–14)

We looked at Esther earlier as a great example of bold womanhood used for godly influence. She remained under the king's authority at all times, yet because of her influence she saved her people. As in Esther's day, we are facing the threat of everything Christian being blotted out. The State commands we bow down and worship it. Just like Esther, if we keep silent, we should not expect to escape just because we're comfortable right now.

There are unusual circumstances in which God has permitted women to lead where there was a lack of male leadership, *e.g.*, Deborah in the book of Judges. We don't have to be in a leadership position to think critically, to vote, to teach our children God's Law and grace, to encourage our husbands in godliness or support his getting involved, or to be an influence to our friends and community. Women need to be involved in politics. Women are doers; they are excellent at getting things done. They are organizers. They are socialites. They are talkers and promoters. They have brilliant administrative skills. They are creative. They are frugal and thrifty. These qualities are invaluable in the realm of politics. A woman can exercise these gifts without having to hold a position of authority or run for office. I believe God is calling women to engage in the political realm and become helpmeets on a corporate level.

Wives and moms are doers. They are proactive and ready to take on challenges. Imagine what we could accomplish, not only in our little corners, but also in the whole world if we start thinking big and long-term! This is something God is waiting to bless! God is so excited when we are committed to the entire Great Commission and ready to *do* something about it!

Next, we'll look at what God thinks about some of the pressing issues of our day. Wives and moms can really excel in this realm!

CHAPTER 11

Left Wing, Right Wing... Am I a Chicken?

or whom will you vote in the next local or national election? Crazy times are upon us. Much is uncertain. Whoever gets your vote will affect the future world in which your kids will live—and don't forget your future grandkids.

As of right now, many of us moms and wives are left hanging, not knowing even what "liberal" or "conservative" means. Are we supposed to sort it all out on our own and then make the right decision? I know many people who don't vote because they don't know for whom to vote! They don't know where they stand personally on the political scale, and they don't know where the candidates stand. It seems that no one has taught us these things.

Many of us get our definitions and ideas about politics from the news, from TV shows, and from our friends. Or maybe we just ask our parents who's getting their vote and then vote the same. This is not acceptable.

This attitude is not loving God with our heart, soul, and mind. Satan just loves this forfeit mentality! If he can convince Christians to go with the flow of what everyone else is saying and doing, he has won a great battle. This is something the church needs to remedy. The church can give an education without actually naming names and telling the congregation "who to vote for." If a church teaches what biblical standards are for any government in any day and age, and the people understand it, there will be no guessing as to where you are on the line. People will figure out who is the best candidate when they have a biblical standard to use for comparison.

Remember: if you are at home changing diapers, making casseroles, and doing schoolwork with your kids, it is important that you make a point to understand this section. This is for you. God wants you to understand this and Satan does not. Satan wants you to think this is irrelevant and does not affect your life. He rejoices when we don't vote. He laughs when we say, "I'm just *Christian*," and then we vote for a president or prime minister whose standards oppose God's standards. I wish I could put big neon flashing lights right here in this chapter! Because when you get a grasp of what God's standard is for today's society, and then act on it (by voting), and then teach your children this same standard, the whole world is going to change! That is why the Bible says, "Resist the devil, and he will flee from you" (James 4:7). The devil will not flee if we do not first resist! It gets tricky though when the lines aren't very clear and we can't see the devil's lies.

Understand this: when it comes to politics, the devil is a wolf in beautiful sheep's wool. Most of the popular political philosophers of our day want you to think that they have your best interests in mind. They are here to take care of you. They are here to make everything fair. They are here to help the poor, the sick, the hurting and dying.

That sounds biblical, right? So then we take their word at face value and we vote for them. For some of us who have home businesses or have husbands who contract out their work, we notice that we sure are paying hefty taxes these days. We notice that we don't have as much money for groceries this month because we had to pay this tax and that tax. But we don't seem to connect the dots. And we always love that "free" money that comes in the mail when the government has decided to give each family a "bonus" or something like that. We think, "Hey, I like free money," and then don't think about it again.

I'm here to burst this bubble! I will give you some very basic principles that come straight out of the Bible. You will be able to use them in any government or society. You can teach this to your kids or your friends. If we say we are Christians, it means we believe the Bible is all-sufficient and without error. It means we believe God has the answers for all of our life's problems. God's Word is where we go to find out how we should live, how we should conduct ourselves, our families, our churches, our businesses, and our civil governments.

Let's start with what goes through many of our minds: "I don't know if I'm conservative or liberal. I don't really know anything about Republican or Democrat. I'm just 'Christian.'" The question now becomes this: "What should a Christian believe when it comes to politics?" As Christians, we instantly have answers because we have an ultimate standard: the Word of God! God has given us very clear boundaries for our government, so all we need to do is check out what they are and then compare modern day political philosophies to that.

God designed government. God is not into making everything equal. Look at His ranks of angels. They all serve His purposes but have different spheres of labor and dominion. Some are higher in authority than others. "Equal rights" as it is understood today is a totally humanistic idea. God says the only thing that is equal about us humans is that we have all fallen short. We all have the equal right to obey! I'm not talking here about race or gender issues. I'm talking about the basic structure of society and God's idea for it.

Why would we live by the world's ideas about hierarchy and ranks of government? We have to take every thought and idea captive *to Christ*. I'm going to show you something very simple here that the world will not want you to see. Satan is working overtime to keep this from Christians. It is the key to taking everything back that belongs to Christ.

God has designed different spheres of government—five of them, in fact. It looks like a triangle or a pyramid. God's government is a bottom-up government. It all starts at the ground level. It does not start at the top and work its way down. That is how the world loves to portray Christianity, but they have it completely backward! Satan's government looks like an upside down triangle or inverted pyramid. He's all about control at the top. Here is the truth. I bet no one taught you this in Sunday school or social studies!

SELF-GOVERNMENT

Self-government is the first and most basic sphere of government. It is the foundation and largest part of the triangle. In a nutshell, self-government means self-control. People who have the character to control themselves do not need very much government over them to control their behavior for them. People who lack the character to control their behavior must be forced to obey by a higher government. Therefore, the more people we have who do not obey God's Laws—starting with the attitudes of their hearts—the more civil government will control our behavior for us.

Does that make sense? The more a society understands and obeys God's standards, the more self-controlled, or self-governed, they will be. That means we will not need as much police or state force to control and govern us.

This is obviously the goal of every Christian. It can be the overall influence of Christianity on an entire nation! Of course, God is the one who ultimately changes our hearts to love His Law, and it is He who gives us the desire to obey. That is why calling the nations to repentance and discipling them is so important if we want to be free of slavery and tyranny. It is also why we need a biblical worldview.

Christians can live moral lives but then go and vote for a president or prime minister who is in opposition to God's Law. Self-government and a biblical worldview should go hand in hand.

Family Government

The second sphere of government is family government. There is God-ordained hierarchy within the family. Though we are all equally members of God's family, He has clearly designated specific roles and divisions of labor within the family structure (1 Cor. 1:1–3). It is not very hard to see the relationship between the breakdown of society and the breakdown of the family. We must get back to God's plan for the family. The church must fight for the family and call its members back to their biblical roles. Here is where the pay-off of self-government begins to show itself. When a person has self-restraint and obeys God's Laws, the family is in proper order. The family is not dysfunctional, but working and productive in society. This is our second building block.

Church Government

The third sphere of government is church government. Individuals make up families. The church is a family of families. That is why in order to have a properly functioning church, you must have a properly functioning family, which means properly functioning individuals. Within the church, we have different functions and divisions of labor as well. All members are parts of the body—with different functions, capabilities, and duties. When church government is in check because its families are in check, look at the community around it! It is like living on a different planet. The church's state of health spills out into the community and marketplace around it.

The Marketplace

The fourth sphere is the marketplace. Businesses seem like they might be in a different category altogether, but if we look at where people spend the majority of their days, we quickly see the importance of this sphere. We only spend a few hours at church each week, at most. People who work outside the home spend anywhere from eight to twelve hours at work every day. If we want to reach the world, we must transform the marketplace. This means getting back to a healthy church, which means healthy families, which means individuals who are self-governing.

Civil Government

The fifth and smallest sphere in God's plan is the civil government. God designed government to keep law-breakers in check. It's to keep them aware of the consequences of disobedience. Imagine you robbed your neighbor's house, and instead of playing golf in a four-star prison cell, you would have to repay your debts by working for this person until you had restored the value of what you took in full, plus more (interest). How many thieves do you think we would have? Surely a lot less. Just think of all the tax dollars that would still be in your wallet instead of paying for steak and mashed potatoes for criminals who never have to pay back the people from whom they stole. This is what God calls "restitution." The bottom line is that when you have a society practicing self-government, the sphere of family government will be in check, and the church will be in check, and then… there is very little need for civil government. Remember, the more a society practices self-control, the less policing they need.

Now that we have established these five spheres of government, we can get into some really basic—but juicy—bits of information that will really help you to sort out what's what in today's society. Simply put, we have God's basic design. Now we need to define some terms and find out where we stand today.

CHAPTER 12

Casseroles, Presidents & Pedicures

I used to be afraid of political talk because it was always so complicated and it sounded kind of scary to me. There's much that still goes totally over my head, but at least now I am equipped with some very basic knowledge to go by. We know God speaks to all areas of life. When it comes to freedom and the future of our country, we have to make it our duty as moms and homemakers to understand some basic political theory! So much is hanging on our knowledge or ignorance of this topic. If you're with me, carry on.

We have observed God's five areas of government, so now we can take a closer look at how God wants us to view civil government. We will base our views not on popular talk shows, news programs, or books. That is not a biblical worldview. We must start on the knowledge that God has revealed what we need to know in Scripture.

LESS IS MORE

The Bible gives two main functions for our civil government: to protect the innocent (and their property) and to punish criminals (Rom. 13:3–4). Who are the innocent? Citizens who obey God's Law. God takes private property seriously. God invented private property. It's all a part of His plan to teach us dominion and stewardship. When God gave the commandment "You shall not steal," that means He has given people areas of private dominion. When someone robs their neighbor, they are actually robbing God. It violates God's rules of personal responsibility and dominion. When we learn how to govern our private belongings, our land, our homes, and especially ourselves by applying God's laws, He will increase the size of our domain, according to His purposes. Here are some important biblical points to consider when we look at government today:

- God does not like centralized power. Centralization occurs when the power of a nation lies in the hands of only a few people. It is "collective." The first major account we have of this happening is the tower of Babel. God did not like this! He scattered them on the earth and confused their languages. He did this to de-centralize their power (Gen. 11:1–8).

- God blesses decentralized government. When the Israelites were in the desert, Moses was dealing with every little problem they had. This was completely inefficient and unproductive, so he appointed judges over groups of tens, hundreds, and thousands. Moses chose the judges according to their *character* (Exod. 18:13–27; Deut. 1:9–16). They were representatives of one ultimate standard: the Law of God. This divided authority into what we can compare today as states or provinces. God granted power to the individual states (tribes) to decide and judge over their own matters. All states/provinces are bound by one constitution—God's Law. Also, in the Bible, each tribe had their own military. There was no one centralized military power. God has given this great biblical model for us. The Ten Commandments are our standard for governing society.

- God is disappointed in nations who want a lot of civil government (1 Sam. 8:10–17). He often gives them what they ask for because big government is a punishment in and of itself. Because we have seen that God's plan is to have maximized self-government and minimized civil government, any time we ask the government to do more for us or take care of us better, it goes against God's plan. We are just like the Israelites when, after God delivered them from Pharaoh, they were still stuck in their slavery mentality and begged to go back to Egypt! We have this same slavery attitude. We don't even know what liberty or freedom is because our allegiance is still with "Pharaoh." We keep turning from God and worshiping false gods (the State). The Bible describes both God and Samuel being upset because the people demanded to have a king like all the other nations. God told Samuel that in asking for this king (big government), they were actually rejecting God Himself! When we desire to have the government take care of everything and tell us what to do, we are replacing God with the State. This is idolatry. God instructed Samuel to warn the people what would happen when they got their king:

> These will be the ways of the king who will reign over you: he will take your sons and appoint them to his chariots and to be his horsemen and to run before his chariots. And he will appoint for himself commanders of thousands and commanders of fifties, and some to plough his ground and to reap his harvest, and to make his implements of war and the equipment of his chariots. He will take your daughters to be perfumers and cooks and bakers. He will take the best of your fields and vineyards and olive orchards and give them to his servants. He will take the tenth of your grain and of your vineyards and give it to his officers and to his servants. He will take your male servants and female servants and the best of your young men and your donkeys, and put them to his work. He will take the tenth of your flocks, and you shall be his slaves. And in that day you will cry out because of your king, whom you have chosen for yourselves, but the LORD will not answer you in that day. (1 Samuel 8:11–18)

This describes children who become slaves, working for the king (civil government). He takes the hard-earned product of labor (our money) that doesn't belong to him, and takes it for himself and his servants (our taxes go to civil government bureaucrats). According to God, the civil government requiring even a ten percent income tax constitutes slavery of the people!

Today we have anywhere between thirty and fifty percent of our earnings taken from us! And because the people wanted this so badly, because they could not and would not govern themselves, when they would cry out to the Lord to take it all back, God said that He would not answer them. Is that a scary thought, or what?

DOWN TO THE NITTY-GRITTY

In today's society, we consider people who are in favor of a big centralized government that holds all the power "left-wing" or "liberal." We consider those in favor of a small, de-centralized government that puts power in the hands of the people, "right-wing" or "conservative." In the end, it's not about right or left, it's about God's standards and our need to obey Him. Wherever that puts us on the world's scale, or whatever name they call it, doesn't matter. The point is that if we are saying we are "just Christian," then we need to be opposed to any kind of big centralized government, and be in favor of a very limited, small civil government—not because we think it's a good idea, but because it is the model God gave us in His Word.

There is no doubt about it—we are in a time of slavery and judgment because we want Pharaoh to take care of us. We want him to give us welfare, to take care of our sick and dying (by giving us "free" healthcare), to feed us, clothe us, and take care of us when we get old (government retirement homes, social security, etc.) Because we have surrendered our personal responsibility to do those things ourselves, Pharaoh is more than happy to do them for us—in exchange for our freedom and our allegiance!

The church is supposed to be the hospital of the world. The church is supposed to care for the poor, the weak, the vulnerable, the widow, and orphan. Because the church stopped doing those things, someone stepped up and said, "I'll do it!" Guess who? Oh yes, power-grabbing government did. The government knows that a people who are dependent on it for their lives are a people who are enslaved to it. It has all the control and power. This is not God's original plan. It is God's judgment.

What we need to do is first repent of our idolatry. We have asked the State to be our god. We have begged the State to provide for and sustain us. We have cried out for the State to make us whole and new, to heal us with its healthcare and with its programs. If this is not idolatry, then what is? We need to repent. If we want out of Egypt, if we want Pharaoh to let us go, we need to start crying out to God to change our slavery mentalities. We need to ask Him to undo all the mental conditioning and training we have received in Pharaoh's boot camp (government school) that taught us to rely on Pharaoh, to pledge allegiance to Pharaoh, and to worship Pharaoh. We must make sure we do not send our children into Pharaoh's training ground where they learn to *love* slavery. The fastest way to achieve this end is to practice self-government, teach your children to do the same, teach them the Law of God, vote in a biblical way, disciple the nations, and be an influence in your church and community.

For some of us, we hear people talking, or we watch the news or read online, and we wonder what they are saying and what certain words mean. It all sounds like Greek to us. We hear stuff about communism or socialism and don't know what the difference is. We hear all this intimidating stuff about economics and think, *That is way over my head*, or *That is irrelevant to my life*. So I will break down in my own words some of the important terms you need to know if you want to be a history-making mom.

FREEDOM

What does freedom really mean? Is it a feeling? Is it being able to do whatever you want? In a Christian worldview, freedom is *the ability to obey God without hindrance or obstacle*. It means we are able to serve God's purpose for us without our sin getting in the way. That is true freedom.

Freedom begins in the spiritual and extends into the natural. In a "free" country, we are essentially a Christian nation, actively obeying God's commands and enjoying the blessings that flow from that obedience. The prosperity and blessing that our nation has experienced is a direct reflection and result of the Christian roots and heritage that started this country. The reason we are losing this prosperity, why our nations are going bankrupt, why government is getting bigger while our freedoms get smaller, is that we have abandoned the basic principles of running our country based on God's standards. The church did not even see it happening because we had our heads in the sand. God's Law equals freedom and prosperity. Man's law equals slavery and tyranny.

TYRANNY

Sometimes we hear this word today, and depending on the particular news station you're listening to or the person you're talking to, it seems to have different meanings. The real definition of tyranny is *rebellion against a God-ordained boundary of government*. We saw that there are five different spheres of government. When one sphere illegally tries to accumulate power within another sphere, tyranny is taking place. When civil government tries to dictate and control the church sphere by telling them what they can or cannot preach from the pulpit, tyranny has taken place. Or when a civil government tells a family they cannot homeschool their children, tyranny has taken place. Tyranny occurs in different ways, so we need to keep a watchful eye at all times and make sure we fight it.

ECONOMICS

The sight of this word might make you yawn. Maybe it's even intimidating. The truth is that we engage in economics every day of our lives. Economics is *the way people use a certain means to attain or acquire certain ends*. It's the study of currency or whatever people value as money. Anything can be considered money if it's valued or considered rare. If we all thought shoelaces were valuable, we could exchange shoelaces for goods and services.

Before money, there was trade. People would trade goods and services for other goods and services. Money, like gold and silver, made trading easier so you could just sell your good or service and then buy what you wanted later. It is convenient. Paper money isn't real money. It is supposed to represent real money that is stored at the bank.

Back in the olden days (but not that long ago), people would take their real gold and silver to the bank. The bank would give them a receipt. This receipt was an official statement saying, "There's really money here." This was convenient because if someone robbed you while traveling, you wouldn't lose all your money since your real money was safe at the bank. That is how we got our paper money. It's only a receipt. The only problem now is… there isn't any real gold or silver at the banks any more. Now all we have is the receipt! It's pretty much fraud. Satan was happy to get off the system of real gold and silver (which happened in the '70s) because he loves to devalue God's stuff. He's the ultimate con artist.

Here's the thing: every single one of us engages in the world's economy on a daily basis. We use the world's money system to buy things, to pay bills, to acquire property. Did you know that God has His own economy? Bet you haven't heard about that at church. Yes, God has His own plan of economics. Right now, the world is not operating on God's economy. It is operating on Satan's counterfeit economy. It's full of fake money that isn't worth anything.

In God's economy, money has real value. It's backed by something real that is valuable like gold or silver. Precious metals are worth something because God made it that way when He created the earth. Because we are right now stuck on the treadmill of the world's counterfeit money system, we're going to have to figure out a way to get back on God's system. We can do this by looking to the Word of God for what He curses and blesses when it comes to the way societies conduct themselves with money.

God has a plan and He wants us to get off the treadmill of the world, programmed at high speed for judgment and destruction. When we operate on God's economic system, it brings prosperity and blessing. Even though we see that the world is receiving a phase of judgment right now for some of this disobedience (like going off real money, which is theft), God wants to prosper His children even during times of famine—just like in Joseph's day!

SOCIALISM

What is socialism? Some of us have never heard this word; others have heard about a "social gospel" or "social justice." These terms are in the same family as the general term "Socialism." *Socialism is the forced redistribution of wealth.* We ask the government to take from the rich and then spread it around to other people who are poor or less well-off. Think of Robin Hood. This confiscation of money goes towards government schools, government housing, welfare, social programs, etc. While there are supporters of socialism who have good intentions (helping less fortunate people), the way in which they are "helping" them is entirely unbiblical. In most cases this form of "helping" is extremely inefficient!

Back in the eighties, the stats showed that for every dollar that went toward these programs, less than thirty cents actually made it to the programs. This means the rest ends up in the hands of government bureaucrats. Charity is a much more effective way of helping people because there are no middle-men to deal with, and a face-to-face approach is the biblical design.

Be assured, socialism is in direct opposition to God's Law of *you shall not steal*. I won't go into all the details, but socialism is a form of communism. Communism wants to get rid of all private property (a *big* no-no in God's Word), and all private ownership (which is God-ordained dominion). It seeks to create a classless society of no rich and no poor. Everyone is equal... equally impoverished! It is strictly a top-down, inverted pyramid government, usually controlled by a dictator.

Socialism—which is a form of communism—seeks to level the playing field in the name of "fairness." It is absolutely everywhere and we don't even notice! We even see this now in the "no child left behind" laws in the U.S. public schools. Instead of having winners or losers, or grading papers with a red pen, everyone gets a trophy and we use more "calming" colors like purple or blue. This is actually a direct attack on God's plan for society. It defies His Law.

Of *course* we need to take care of the poor and help the needy. Don't worry: God has a specific plan for all that—and it doesn't involve the government confiscating our money.

CAPITALISM

Boy, people toss this around with some seriously negative baggage these days. Documentaries by people like Michael Moore have misled thousands of people all across our nation. Everyone seems to think that capitalism is bad, and we need to be more like Europe. Guess what, folks—Europe is broke! Instead of getting our definitions and opinions from popular documentaries or celebrities, we need to look at what this word really means and how we should view it in light of God's Word.

Capitalism is *private ownership of property, production, goods, labor, and resources*. So instead of the government (or Pharaoh) owning these things, individuals own these things and govern over them themselves. It's godly stewardship. It's dominion.

Now why on earth does this word get such a bad rap these days? Well, for one, the media, news stations, and TV shows are all on a socialism bandwagon as we speak. Hollywood oozes with people blatantly against capitalism and have no problem speaking out about it. Celebrities keep talking about "evil capitalism." That makes me want to ask them this question: "Excuse me, could I please have that gorgeous leather couch of yours? We're much poorer than you are, so since you believe everything should be 'fair', I would really like that leather couch in your living room. Maybe throw in those lamps too… And that diamond ring, if you don't mind. You have plenty, after all."

In addition to the mainstream media bashing capitalism, the public schools strategically teach gullible kids that it is evil. (I should know! I sat in a public school history class which taught that capitalism is bad and socialism is good.) Curriculum writers and others know that if they can indoctrinate the youth, they have won over an entire generation.

The truth of the matter is that capitalism—when uninhibited by the government—promotes an environment of entrepreneurship and creativity. When the government is not involved in regulating our businesses and taxing us to death, it allows for healthy competition, which makes our groceries cheaper, our health costs cheaper… not to mention those shoes! Capitalism is an economic system that allows payoff for personal responsibility, character and diligence. That payoff is called *profit*. Of course, no one can guarantee your success. There is always risk involved, but in a capitalistic system, the possibility is there! This is why immigrants from all over the world came to our country: for the opportunity to succeed. They did not have this opportunity in their homeland because there the government was so heavily regulating businesses, and taxing the people at such high rates, no one could prosper! They had to come to America to get that opportunity.

Capitalism promotes the biblical idea of private ownership of property and goods. That means being able to set your own prices on that homemade jewelry you crafted and then sold on eBay.

Are there people out there who seek something beyond capitalism? Yes, there are people who seek what we call a *monopoly*. They want to own everything and control it and be the richest people in the world. They want power. This is nothing more than old-fashioned greed. Always keep in mind that these are specific individuals with evil intentions. Capitalism in and of itself is not evil. At its core, it promotes very biblical ideas.

FREE MARKET

We don't often hear this word from the pulpit. For some reason, pastors seem to skip this topic and move right along to something more "inspirational." A free market or free enterprise system goes hand in hand with capitalism.

A free market is *the ability to buy, sell, and exchange goods and services, or trade—without government intervention.* The government is greedy. The government doesn't have any money, only we people do. The government finds ways to take a little here, take a little there, and steal a little here, pickpocket a little there in the form of hefty taxes. Remember, God told Samuel that at a ten percent tax, the people were now in slavery! The government also likes to dictate the prices we set for our goods, or what our bottom price must be, just to be "fair" to everyone else. What that does is cuts out healthy competition and forces everything to be more expensive. The Bible forbids government to control trade or the exchanging of goods (Rev. 13:19). The only thing government should do when it comes to the marketplace is protect people from coercion or fraud, protect private property, and punish criminals (Rom. 13:3–4).

The free market works on the principle of supply and demand. Say I want a pedicure. Someone provides the service of pedicures. They set a price. If I think the price is too high, I can go somewhere else. If I pay for the pedicure, I have agreed that their price was a fair price for the service they provided. I walk out of the nail shop with spiffy feet and they make a profit. Win-win. When the government stays out of the business arena, everything gets cheaper, including the cost of living. People in the pedicure business have to have better quality pedicures, because the word will get around that the little shop on the corner has the *best* pedicures in town *and* the lowest prices. As a result, that business gets more clients and the clients are happier.

This is a healthy system. If the government decides all nail shops have to have a minimum charge of $35 per pedicure, you can guarantee the customer service will be terrible and the quality of the pedicures will not be good. You'll come out of there with messed up, gooey nails, and they won't even care. Because why should they have to care? They know you can go anywhere you like and it's not going to be any cheaper. No one is motivated to give you a great pedicure experience! In a free market, the government stays out of the way, and the business owner decides the quality and price of the service. He is motivated to do business with you! Therefore, you get a great pedicure and he can pay his bills and make a profit.

INFLATION

I find it rather insane that lip-gloss costs $20 at the drug store, or that it costs $7 for a gallon of organic milk. Is that insanely expensive, or is it just me? What is inflation? It's something that happens to a balloon, right? Or water-wings we put on our kids when they go swimming at the pool. Well, very similar to the effect of blowing up a balloon, inflation means to make something appear bigger than it is. In our economy, inflation means *to artificially increase the money supply*. Simply put, the government thinks that it can print money as if it's a game of Monopoly and then put it into circulation (or nowadays, just increase numbers in a computer). This makes it appear as though we have more money in America. But do we really?

When we add too much flour to our cookie dough recipe, it decreases the power of the baking soda or baking powder. The cookies will be tough and they just don't rise because the baking soda has less of an effect. The same is true when the government prints money that isn't really there. It decreases the actual value of the dollar. As a result, the dollar will buy less. A dollar that used to be able to buy a box of Hamburger Helper will now buy only one jellybean.

So when we say that the housing market is inflated, that is only a result of the government putting fake money (also called *fiat* money) into circulation that doesn't really exist. It decreases the purchasing power of each dollar, which means the price of housing has to go up in order to compensate for the loss of actual value. God calls this theft!

Another way to describe what has happened is "debasing the currency." Before the paper dollar, people used precious metals, like gold and silver, to exchange goods and services. Gold and silver is valued because it is somewhat rare. It is also transportable. You can divide it up, you can melt it, use it for other purposes (like dental fillings). Gold and silver are what we call "hard currency" because they are actually worth something.

Our paper money is not actually worth anything: it is paper. It is supposed to *represent* real gold and silver. Now we have digital money that has nothing behind it. They are just digits. If the digits represented something real, it would be okay. I have nothing against technology, because God is the Creator of technology, but the way we have set up the modern system, it is bound to collapse. You cannot base an economy on fake money or numbers in a computer. There is nothing supporting it. It's just pretend. That kind of economy will collapse.

Before we had this paper money (which was, remember, once a bank receipt saying there was real gold or silver in the bank) there were coins.

People would sometimes try to cheapen the precious metal coins by mixing it with baser metals and trying to pass it off as real gold or silver. Can you say *knock-off*? If we print our own fake money at home and try to pass it off as the real thing, police call it "counterfeiting" and we will go to jail. When the government does it by printing more money or adding more numbers (credit) into the system, they say it's perfectly legal! God says it's theft (Isa. 1:22; Amos 8:5). Theft will not be blessed. A society that bases its whole economy on fake money and theft invites total ruin.

STATISM

Statism is *the practice of giving the government unlimited powers*. Socialism and communism fall into this category. Any kind of dictatorship or centralized, big government falls into this category. It gives the State the power of "God": to give; to take away; to control the lives of people. The State seeks to be sovereign and rule over the affairs of man. As we saw before, it is idolatry. Only the Creator of the universe has any right to do those things. God calls for a State with very limited power. When the State tries to "be God," it will bring upon itself cursing and destruction. And there's your happy thought for the day.

AUTONOMY

Now there's a strange-looking word. Guess what—it's all around us. It's on TV, it lives next door to you, it has diseased our government, and is promoted everywhere.

Autonomy means *self-law*. It is the belief and practice of determining the standards (or truths) of life for yourself. It replaces God's Law with your own. It's man's law.

There are only two options. It will be one or the other. Either you follow God's standard of truth or you follow man's. When you hear someone say "Well, that's true for you, but not for me," that is code for "I follow my own laws because I am the god of my own universe. I have rejected the God of the Bible and His standards. I worship me." When you hear the *true for you, but not for me* line, you might want to step to the side—you don't want to get in the path of the lightning bolt that's on its way.

Man-made, man-centered law is, in its simplest form, idolatry. If you've ever read the Bible, you know how serious a crime idolatry is to God. Humanism falls into this category. When we refer to secular humanism, you know it's bad. Autonomy and secular humanism worship man as supreme. Man decides what is right and wrong, and they reject God's Law altogether.

THEONOMY

Theonomy is the opposite of autonomy. While autonomy means *self-law*, theonomy means *God's Law*. We already know that you can pick only one. You can serve only one master. Either God's Law is the standard for right and wrong, or man's law is. There are consequences for both. One requires accountability and results in either blessing or cursing. The other requires nothing but an imagination and results in damnation. You pick.

Another thing to remember is that all law is religious, even if it is secular law or it claims to be "neutral" or "non-religious." Remember, there is no neutrality. All law presupposes someone in charge, deciding a standard of ethics: what is right and what is wrong. It is either God or man. Because of this, all societies are theocracies: a government ruled by a god or deity. If man rules it, we are committing idolatry—that is, worshipping man as god.

By the way, God's Law has always existed and always will. Murder did not suddenly become wrong when God gave Moses the Ten Commandments on Mount Sinai. Murder of innocent people has always been wrong because it contradicts God's character. Anything that contradicts God's character, which is His standard, is sin.

The goal of every Christian is to apply theonomy in his own life, to teach it to his children, practice it in his church, and teach the community how to obey it. That is how you disciple nations. You start by discipling communities.

These are only a few key definitions that are important for every world-changing mom and wife to know. Become familiar with these. You will need them. There is one last tool I'd like to give you in this chapter—five questions by which you can find out the basic nature of any society.

Who's in charge here? This answers the question of *sovereignty*. Is God in charge? Is the constitution in charge? Is a dictator in charge?

To whom do I report? This answers the question of *representation*. Do we answer to man? God? The police? The government?

What are the rules? This will tell you about whose *law* is enforced—God's or man's?

What happens to me if I obey (or disobey)? This is about *sanctions*—the spheres and limitations of government we talked about earlier.

Does this have a future? This will tell you about the *legacy* this society will leave. It's about inheritance. Will our children inherit a blessing or a curse?

If you fully understand these concepts—the whole world is on its way to turning upside down… in a good way. This is really the key to changing everything: a biblical worldview. There is not a single crack or crevice in this life over which God is not sovereign, over which He doesn't have dominion and power, and that He hasn't come to redeem.

Here is where the world starts to change—on the battleground of your mind. The fear of the Lord is the beginning of knowledge. Knowledge is power. When you start to digest this full course meal of meat and potatoes and you start cooking it up for your family and friends, and after they wipe that look of shock off their faces, watch how God starts to work in them. This will involve stirring pots. You are going to have to be a pot-stirrer—not someone who chucks unmentionables at fans, but a pot-stirrer. This message is not popular, but it's godly. He will bless your efforts when you conform your thoughts to His. He will increase your domain as you prove that you are ready to bring Jesus into every part of life, instead of retreating from it and allowing the enemy to have control.

We fight the battle here on earth. The blessing is also here on earth. The Kingdom is here on earth. It's amazing the persecution some of us will have to endure for defending these truths even within our own circle of influence. Some of your best friends might think you are a lunatic. They might call you a heretic and they probably have no idea what they are saying. If that happens to you, be comforted and know that the truths presented in this chapter are truths the church has stood by for thousands of years. It is only now that the church is so conformed to the world that it has lost its ability to discern good from evil.

So be ready for it. Equip yourself with the armor of God. Pray every day. Commit yourself to learning more. I pray God gives you the hunger to continue to dig much deeper into the issues that I am touching on so lightly.

Coming up next is the exciting, heart-pounding future of the world… that does not include the words *doom* and *gloom*!

CHAPTER 13

The Whole Lump of ~~Carbs~~ Dough

You are about to read one of the most important questions you can ask yourself. Your answer defines your whole life's existence. It will change your life and all the lives around you. It will change the course of the future.

Is Jesus reigning now? Will Jesus reign only at the end of days, after He defeats Satan and throws him into the pit? Has Jesus established the Kingdom yet? Or does Jesus usher in the Kingdom at the end of time? We have all heard different things about this. I want to set the record straight. As I said, our answer about this defines our whole life's existence.

The answer is in Scripture and starts with John. John the Baptizer went around preaching, "Repent, for the kingdom of heaven is at hand" (Matt. 3:2). That is interesting, don't you think? After John was arrested, Jesus took his exact message and began preaching the same thing, "Repent, for the kingdom of heaven is at hand" (Matt. 4:17). Then Jesus instructs His disciples to preach this message also (Matt. 10:7). Now what does "at hand" mean? Did Jesus mean, "The kingdom will be here in 2,000 more years?" If we look at all the other ways Scripture uses the term "at hand" in both the Old and New Testaments, we see that it means "near" or "shortly." It means just what you'd think it means. John, the disciples, and Jesus announced that the Kingdom of Heaven was about to be established to a greater degree than it had been previously.

It wasn't as though up until this point there was no Kingdom of God and now there would be. It meant that in Jesus' death and resurrection, the Kingdom would come into full fruition! We know God has always had a Kingdom here on earth. Not a political kingdom, but a spiritual kingdom that embodies believers both spiritually and physically, which then carries out into their daily lives. The Kingdom shines into everything, including politics, businesses, and families.

My dad pointed out to me once that God has always been a God of the *now*. God said to Moses, "I Am that I Am," not "I Was" or "I Will Be"… but "I Am." Jesus is sitting on a throne in heaven right *now*, directing the course of history *now*, and interacting with all His creation on a personal level *now*. He is *here*. Gary DeMar pointed this out further in an article:

> Even Nebuchadnezzar understood that God's "dominion is an everlasting dominion, and His kingdom endures from generation to generation" (Dan. 4:34). There is no "parenthesis," no gap of nearly two thousand years where God's "dominion" has somehow been put on hold . . . it is equally obvious that the New Testament describes an approaching kingdom: "The kingdom of God is at hand" (Mark 1:14–15; cf. Matt. 4:12–17). This means that there is a fuller expression of that already present glorious kingdom approaching as God takes on human flesh and personally oversees the kingdom that brings with it the once-for-all sacrifice promised so long ago to Adam and Eve.[1]

We have absolute assurance that the Kingdom of God is already established. Jesus made this even clearer when He put out the challenge to His critics: "If I cast out demons by the Spirit of God, surely the kingdom of God has come upon you" (Matt. 12:28). We know Jesus cast out demons by the Spirit of God; therefore, the Kingdom had come upon them!

This is exciting for those of us who have been thinking for years that Jesus won't establish His kingdom until the end of the world.

We've Been Ripped Off

When I learned this, I felt totally ripped off. I realized all this time I had believed Jesus wasn't really reining yet. I was missing a whole level of Christ's authority and dominion. You see, somewhere along the line, I had been taught that God's Kingdom exists only in the spiritual realm of heaven and angels. I thought the physical realm, including all our earthly governments, are of another kingdom: the kingdom of Satan. Somehow I had come to believe that this world belonged to the devil; that it was rightfully Satan's domain. The great deceiver is the "god of this world" and he owns and controls everything, right? Is this really true? If Jesus is the King of kings and Lord of lords, and His domain applies only to the spiritual realm, that would mean He has no right to tell the king of this earthly realm (Satan) what to do. It also means that when they make public prayer to God illegal, or when they want to take everything Christian out of the laws of the land, or even wipe out Christianity, it would mean they have every right to do so "under the order of King Satan, the rightful king of this earthly realm."

Does that sound backward to you? I hope so, because it's a lie! The Bible does refer to Satan as "the god of this world," but we must seek to understand what it means by that. We will get into this later, but I will quickly touch on it now. "The god of this world" is referring to the counterfeit world system Satan has set up in order to deceive the nations. Satan is not the literal god of the *cosmos*. Only the Creator of the cosmos is the God of the cosmos. God has a Kingdom—the real Kingdom—and Satan has a counterfeit kingdom.

Satan does not rule over the earth. God does, and He has representatives to act as ministers of his reign: us! Christians rule over the earth as God's stewards (Gen. 1:28; Matt. 28: 18–20). We are to care for the created order. We are to govern and uphold the created order to the standards the real King of kings has set for us. That means Christians are to declare God's rightful ownership in every area of life, from pizza delivery to care of the environment, to science and art and media.

We are to be the representatives of the Kingdom, which is both spiritual and physical. God doesn't have two separate kingdoms. There's only one. It is all encompassing and comprehensive. God's Kingdom extends over all His creation, in every dimension, sphere, space, and time—not just the heavens. When Jesus said, "My Kingdom is not of this world," in John 18:36, notice He didn't say, "My Kingdom is not *on* or *in* this world." He said *of* which describes *from where* His power *originates*. Jesus' power does not come from the earthly realm, but it extends throughout it!

Where Is Jesus Now?

If Jesus is reigning now, what does He plan on doing from now until Judgment Day? Well, there is no mystery here. The Bible speaks plainly. Jesus ascended to heaven and was seated at the right hand of God. David prophesied this event: "The LORD said to my Lord, 'Sit at My right hand, till I make Your enemies Your footstool'" (Ps. 110:1). In other words, the Father said to the Son that He would remain seated at His right hand—reigning—until all His enemies have been humbled under His feet. Wow. What a revolutionary scripture! In fact, the whole passage of Psalm 110 describes how mighty and powerful Jesus is during His reign. Do you understand the magnitude of this verse? Jesus must reign from heaven until He has put all His enemies under His feet—on earth! This means we can safely conclude that Jesus is not coming back to a world dominated by Satan! It means Jesus is returning to a Kingdom that fully submits to Him and is free of enemies! This is so amazing. What a promise. How far will the Kingdom reach? How vast will it be? Let's look at a few scriptures that give us the promise of Christ's victory here on planet Earth.

> *Of the increase of His government and of peace there will be no end, on the throne of David and over his kingdom, to establish it and to uphold it with justice and with righteousness from this time forth and forevermore. The zeal of the* Lord *of hosts will do this.* (Isaiah 9:7)
>
> *The earth will be full of the knowledge of the* Lord *as the waters cover the sea.* (Isaiah 11:9)
>
> *All the ends of the earth will remember and turn to the* Lord*, and all the families of the nations will bow down before Him.* (Psalm 22:27)
>
> *And to Him was given dominion and glory and a kingdom, that all peoples, nations, and languages should serve Him; His dominion is an everlasting dominion,* which shall not pass away, *and His kingdom one that* shall not be destroyed. (Daniel 7:14)

There are dozens and dozens of verses and passages that confirm these promises. We see that God's Kingdom will "increase" and that it will result in peace that has no end. By the way, peace does not mean *the absence of conflict*. God's kind of peace means *victory in the **presence** of conflict*. We see that there will come a time in world history when the knowledge of the Lord fills the whole earth. This is not taking place in heaven; otherwise, it would say, "The heavens will be full of the knowledge of the Lord."

The Psalms overflow with passages that speak of the temporary rebellion of man towards God, God overcoming them, and then great prosperity and peace throughout the world for His faithful people who keep His covenant. We also have Jesus' parables about what history will look like for the Kingdom of God:

> *He put another parable before them, saying, "The Kingdom of heaven is like a grain of mustard seed that a man took and sowed in his field. It is the smallest of all seeds, but when it has grown it is larger than all the garden plants and becomes a tree, so that the birds of the air come and make nests in its branches."* (Matthew 13:31–32)

When Jesus came to earth, He had only twelve disciples. Look at how they turned the whole world upside down! It started small, but was like a growing tidal wave... and it will continue to rise throughout time and history! The Kingdom will start out small and continue to grow until it affects everything around it. This parable says that the birds of the air come to the tree for refuge. This is what the Kingdom has in store for the world. The enemies of God will not prevail; instead, the church will become the answer to which the world turns. Does this sound a little different from what you learned? Doesn't it make you excited about the future God has for us? Jesus gave another parable just so we wouldn't miss His point:

> *The Kingdom of Heaven is like the yeast a woman used in making bread. Even though she put only a little yeast in three measures of flour, it permeated every part of the dough.* (Matthew 13:33)

An Interesting Comparison

Jesus couldn't make it any clearer for us. The Kingdom of God is going to permeate the earth! It's going to affect every part of life here in history. But like the dough, it requires kneading. A baker's website describes the science behind yeast and how it makes bread rise:

> Kneading is a necessary step in the bread-making process. The biggest problem bakers have is they don't knead the dough long enough. . . . As you knead dough, many important things take place: the gluten becomes developed so the bread can rise to its fullest. Air bubbles are incorporated into the dough necessary for the dough's rise and the ingredients are redistributed for the yeast to feed on, resulting in a more active fermentation. This enables the dough to expand to its fullest during the rising and baking steps.[2]

I thought it was an interesting thing that Jesus compared the Kingdom to bread-making. Notice this article says most people don't knead the dough long enough. I think that really sums up our modern-day thinking about the Kingdom of God. We are very short sighted. We don't realize that the expansion of the Kingdom is gradual and takes time. It takes some physical labor and commitment to the end result. If you've ever made bread by hand, you know your arms get a workout. It's not the easiest task. But—oh, boy! That fresh loaf of bread out of the oven with butter on it sure makes it worth all the work! It's heaven in your mouth!

I also thought it was interesting how the website described that the gluten must develop so the bread can rise to its fullest. That is also a great illustration of the importance of our maturity as Christians in order for the Kingdom to expand. If we don't fully develop and mature, the Kingdom doesn't expand. If we don't know how to interpret the information our brain receives through the mind of Christ, if we are immature in our theology, and if we don't have the skill of discernment, the Kingdom does not expand. If we are not equipped to dismantle and demolish every argument that sets itself up against God, the Kingdom does not expand.

The under-developed yeast causes the loaf of bread to collapse. Here's an interesting observation: "Air bubbles are incorporated into the dough necessary for the dough's rise." I like to think of these air bubbles as the trials, tribulations, pain, and pressures we go through in life. Every Christian goes through a "kneading" process. Sometimes it happens on a personal level and sometimes on a national, corporate level. Pressure and pain reveals in us our true motives. It reveals what is really in our hearts. It causes us to grow. We don't always understand why God allows certain atrocities in life, but we can be comforted in knowing that it all serves God's purpose in one way or another.

R. J. Rushdoony wrote, "Nothing happens that will not further God's Kingdom and the glory ultimately of His people in Him and to His purpose." This gives us hope that we should never give up on the long-term goal of seeing the knowledge of the Lord full in the earth as the waters cover the sea, even when times look bad. The air bubbles in life—the trials believers go through—are all for God's sovereign purpose and it will bring Him ultimate glory.

> *Consider it all joy, my brethren, when you encounter various trials, knowing that the testing of your faith produces endurance.* (James 1:1–3)

This verse makes a lot more sense when you read it with a long-term vision in mind. The testing of our faith produces endurance… endurance for what? Why would we need endurance if God is going to rapture us out of the earth? We wouldn't need that character quality unless God has a whole lot to accomplish on earth that requires diligence, faithfulness, and long-suffering: endurance. Some translations say "steadfastness" or "perseverance" and even "patience." They all describe the need to continue on, and that requires long-term vision. Air bubbles cause something else to happen in the loaf: "Ingredients are redistributed for the yeast to feed on, resulting in a more active fermentation."

We can also look at air bubbles as God's way of conditioning us through direct opposition and head-on challenges to our faith. For example, God may use things like communism or humanism as ways to smarten up His people. Because those two ideas are so prevalent in the world and have worked their way into the church, (Satan has his own lump of dough), it will either cause Christians to fall into a greater slumber where they will invoke God's wrath upon them, or it will cause them to wake up and smell the coffee! It will cause the church to stop wimping around and finally take action. It results in a more "active fermentation."

The article said: "This enables the dough to expand to its fullest during the rising and baking steps." The Kingdom is like a little yeast in a big lump of dough that works into the whole lump until it permeates the whole thing. The process includes God kneading and working the dough in various ways. Air bubbles like trials, tribulations, and direct confrontations are worked into the dough for the betterment of the long-term outcome. The result is that the dough (the Kingdom) expands and rises "to its fullest."

Jesus paints a very clear picture about what we can expect for the Kingdom of God here on earth! Satan is not going to overcome the world or rule God's Kingdom here, anytime, anywhere. The bread does not collapse in on itself. Rather, Jesus tells us how much authority He has, since His resurrection:

> *"All authority in heaven and on earth has been given to me."*

Jesus overcame sin, death, and Satan. He now has absolute dominion over both heaven and earth. We are Christ's ambassadors. We now reign with Him here on earth and govern over it. That is why He gave us the Great Commission. It is a commission that involves authority through Christ:

> *"Therefore go and make disciples of all nations, baptizing them in the name of the Father and of the Son and of the Holy Spirit, and teaching them to obey everything I have commanded you. And surely I am with you always, to the very end of the age."*

Jesus didn't say, "Go and witness to the nations," or "Go and preach to the nations." He said, "Make disciples of all nations." This is a completely different idea. Witnessing is just one little aspect, one little slice of the pie. Discipleship involves teaching—explaining to others how to obey God's Law. This is what will cause worldwide prosperity. Even unbelievers who obey God's Law will prosper from it.

This concept is similar to immigrants who live in our country. They don't get to vote or run for office, but they experience the benefits of our freedoms and the laws that protect them.

God's Law equals liberation. God's Law restrains our carnal natures and gives us all the principles by which nations should live to be successful. Jesus goes even further. Not only will His church expand and fill the earth, making disciples of all nations, but the church actually goes on the attack! The church is no wimp in the world. It is not "nice" in the sense that it is not neutral. It goes from defensive to offensive: "And I tell you, you are Peter, and on this rock I will build my church, and the gates of hell shall not prevail against it" (Matt. 16:18).

The gates of hell shall not prevail against *what?* The Church! The gates of Hades are there for defense. This means the church is attacking at the gates. I've heard it said before: "No one has ever seen gates attack anyone." Gates don't attack people, but Jesus says the Church will. And it will prevail!

The Scripture That Changed My World

While there are hundreds of other passages I could cite here supporting all this, I'd like to focus on one particular passage that really changed my whole perspective on the future. It is the account of Daniel interpreting King Nebuchadnezzar's dream (found in Daniel 2:31–45). He first proves that he is a real prophet by telling the king what it was he dreamed:

> *You saw, O king, and behold, a great image. This image, mighty and of exceeding brightness, stood before you, and its appearance was frightening. The head of this image was of fine gold, its chest and arms of silver, its middle and thighs of bronze, its legs of iron, its feet partly of iron and partly of clay. As you looked, a stone was cut out by no human hand, and it struck the image on its feet of iron and clay, and broke them in pieces. Then the iron, the clay, the bronze, the silver, and the gold, all together were broken in pieces, and became like the chaff of the summer threshing floors; and the wind carried them away, so that not a trace of them could be found. But the stone that struck the image became a great mountain and filled the whole earth.*

Then Daniel interprets the dream:

> *You, O king, the king of kings, to whom the God of heaven has given the kingdom, the power, and the might, and the glory, and into whose hand he has given, wherever they dwell, the children of man, the beasts of the field, and the birds of the heavens, making you rule over them all—you are the head of gold. Another kingdom inferior to you shall arise after you, and yet a third kingdom of bronze, which shall rule over all the earth. And there shall be a fourth kingdom, strong as iron, because iron breaks to pieces and shatters all things. And like iron that crushes, it shall break and crush all these. And as you saw the feet and toes, partly of potter's clay and partly of iron, it shall be a divided kingdom, but some of the firmness of iron shall be in it, just as you saw iron mixed with the soft clay. And as the toes of the feet were partly iron and partly clay, so the kingdom shall be partly strong and partly brittle. As you saw the iron mixed with soft clay, so they will mix with one another in marriage, but they will not hold together, just as iron does not mix with clay. And in the days of those kings the God of heaven will set up*

> *a kingdom that shall never be destroyed, nor shall the kingdom be left to another people. It shall break in pieces all these kingdoms and bring them to an end, and it shall stand forever, just as you saw that a stone was cut from a mountain by no human hand, and that it broke in pieces the iron, the bronze, the clay, the silver, and the gold. A great God has made known to the king what shall be after this. The dream is certain, and its interpretation sure.*

Daniel tells the king that this statue represents political empires. He informs the king that he represents the head of gold on the statue. The chest and arms of silver was the Medo-Persian Empire that would conquer them. The middle and thighs of bronze represented the Grecian empire that conquered the Medo-Persian Empire. Finally, the legs of iron represented the Roman Empire. The feet and toes describe that it would be a divided kingdom—partly strong, partly brittle. Then comes the exciting part: it describes that during the days of the Roman Empire, "The God of heaven will set up a kingdom that shall never be destroyed, nor shall the kingdom be left to another people." This is describing the advent of Jesus! He prophesied that Jesus would set up a new kingdom that would destroy all those kingdoms and "bring them to an end, and it shall stand forever." Jesus was the stone that was cut from the mountain, but not by a human hand. In the earlier part of the passage when Daniel first described what the king saw, he said that the stone that struck the statue became a mountain and filled the whole earth.

This fits so nicely with the parables Jesus gave us about the mustard seed and the yeast in the dough. It starts small (the stone) and becomes huge (a mountain that fills the whole earth).

I don't know if this is new to you or not, but this turned my whole world upside down! We can see so clearly that the whole message of the Bible is that Jesus triumphs in human history! The Kingdom is a slow-growing—but ever-expanding—Kingdom. It will not be crushed; rather, it is the church that will do the crushing. We will "crush Satan under our feet" (Rom. 16:20).

CHAPTER 14

The End is Near... or Far?

> *Eschatology is inseparable from purpose—purpose in history. The goal of the enemy is the Kingdom of Man. The goal of Christ's people must be the Kingdom of God, ruled by God's Law-Word. Eschatology is not only about ends, but also means to the given goal. This is why theonomy, God's law and its rule, is inseparable from God's Kingdom.*[1]

Popular prophecy books paint the future in a light that makes Satan triumphant and Jesus a loser—at least for a time. Jesus is not a loser in history! He is victorious, never giving up His authority over the earth to Satan. Jesus is presently reigning from heaven and has all authority in heaven and earth. He will come back for a victorious Bride:

> *[Christ] gave up His life for her to make her holy and clean, washed by the cleansing of God's word. He did this to present her to Himself as a glorious church without a spot or wrinkle or any other blemish. Instead, she will be holy and without fault.* (Ephesians 5:25–27)

Is the church without spot or blemish? Ha! The church is crawling with corruption as we speak. This means we have a long, long way to go before Christ will be presenting His Bride to Himself as perfect. This will require our reforming ourselves to be like Christ again. This means we must have a biblical worldview by which we think and act in every detail. This will require a refiner's fire: trials, tribulations, and sacrifice. The church will need to return to loving the Law and preaching the Law and obeying the Law, as well as singing the victorious Psalms as it used to. Right now, we're stuck on emotional "me-centered" worship tunes that glorify and emphasize our feelings instead of glorifying Christ's triumph and dominion over the world. David Chilton made an important observation about the content of our worship songs and our view of eschatology:

> There is a very important connection between the Church's *worldview* and the Church's *hymns*. If your heart and mouth are filled with songs of victory, you will tend to have an eschatology of dominion; if, instead, your songs are fearful, expressing a longing

for escape—or if they are weak, childish ditties—your worldview and expectations will be escapist and childish.

Historically, the *basic* hymnbook for the Church has been the Book of Psalms. The largest book of the Bible is the Book of Psalms, and God providentially placed it right in the middle of the Bible, so that we couldn't miss it! Yet how many churches use the Psalms in musical worship? It is noteworthy that *the Church's abandonment of dominion eschatology coincided with the Church's abandonment of the Psalms.*

The Psalms are inescapably Kingdom-oriented. They are full of conquest, victory, and the dominion of the saints. They remind us constantly of the warfare between God and Satan, they incessantly call us to do battle against the forces of evil, and they promise us that we shall inherit the earth. When the Church sang the Psalms—not just little snatches of them, but *comprehensively*, through the *whole* Psalter—she was strong, healthy, aggressive, and could not be stopped. That is why the devil has sought to keep us from singing the Psalms, to rob us of our inheritance. If we are to recapture the eschatology of dominion, we must reform the Church; and a crucial aspect of that reformation should be a return to the singing of Psalms.[2]

What we have just learned about a growing Kingdom may leave you wondering about all the popular End Times stuff that we see everywhere. If the truth is that the Kingdom of God is expanding and growing over the course of history, how is it that so many books and videos keep coming out with the underlying message that the earth is Satan's domain? I think we have fallen into the slumber that Jesus talks about in the parable of the weeds:

> *The Kingdom of heaven may be compared to a man who sowed good seed in his field, but while his men were sleeping, his enemy came and sowed weeds among the wheat and went away. So when the plants came up and bore grain, then the weeds appeared also.* (Matthew 13:24–25)

THE BOOK OF *REVELATION*... OR OF *SECRETS*?

Because we have been more committed to entertainment and obsessed with the mysterious rather than with sound doctrine, we have allowed our imaginations, instead of the Bible, to direct our theology. Plus, exciting end-times scenarios sell tons of books. It seems Christians are spiritual adrenaline junkies. We are totally hooked on the mysterious. Much New Age theology has crept in and has us caught up in "the mystical things of God." But guess what? The Bible is the *revealed* Word of God, not the *mysterious* Word of

God. There certainly are things that only God knows and we will have to wait and find out one day—after all, the secret things belong to Him—but in general, God means for us to understand His Word so we may act upon it in faith. It seems that when it comes to the study of End Times, we seem to think that the book of Revelation is supposed to stay a giant mystery that no one can crack. The late Dr. Greg Bahnsen described the way many modern Christians have become accustomed to this train of thought:

> God did not give us the book of Revelation to make us stand back and ask "What on earth could that mean? I guess we will just have to leave it to the guys who are preaching," and then close our Bibles and go away. God wants us to understand this. God wants us to read His Word and get the benefit that He intends from that Word. That is why, along the way, He explains what this book is all about. The book [Revelation] is not really all that difficult to put together. Particular sections or images may be hard for us, but overall we can see what the book of Revelation is all about. Of course the book is going to undoubtedly be troublesome if we try to read it for something it does not intend to be. If we take out our instructions for putting together a bicycle, and try to read it according to the same principles as poetry, then we are not going to make a whole lot of sense out of putting the bicycle together. Likewise, if we think reading a last will and testament is the same as reading the TV Guide, and we try to apply principles for the TV Guide to the will, then we are not going to be able to make any sense of it. If we do not come to the book of Revelation with respect for the kind of literature it is, then of course it is going to be nonsense to us.
>
> To put it simply, the book of Revelation is highly figurative literature. There are visions and symbols and so forth. What often happens is that Christians—in fact there is a whole school of thought that has become famous for doing this—go to the book of Revelation as though it is a newspaper account written ahead of time. Then from the newspaper account they build their charts and do all that sort of thing. Is the book of Revelation written like a newspaper? No. Is it a report similar to what you might read in *The New York Times*? Of course not. The book of Revelation is very figurative. It has a lot of imagery and a lot of symbols.[3]

When it comes to the future of the world, Christians often make the mistake of trying to decipher single verses out of the Bible. We pick one here and there and invent a whole theory based on those one or two verses taken out of context!

People are obsessed with trying to interpret the Bible "literally." That is impossible. No one interprets the Bible that way. Otherwise, we would have to believe that Psalm 91:4 says that God is really a chicken: "He will cover you with His feathers, and under His wings you will find refuge..." To interpret the Bible "literally" should mean that we interpret it *according to the type of literature it is*. Is it poetry? Is it a historical genealogy? Is it a parable? Is it highly figurative? You cannot read the whole Bible in one way and expect to make sense of it.

In addition, instead of taking a verse here and a verse there and formulating an end-times theology around them, we should look at the Bible as one whole message. What is the story of the Bible from Genesis to Revelation? It is about the redemption of the created order, the lifting of the curse, and the expansion of God's Kingdom on earth. There is much in that story as to how it was and is to be accomplished, from the Fall to the Flood, to the Birth and Resurrection of Christ, to the Great Commission and finally Christ returning to a Bride "without spot or blemish." The whole message of the Bible is calling man to repentance and responsibility to expand the Kingdom.

The story of the Bible is not all about some Antichrist, but that sure seems to be a focus in pop Christian culture. Why does this matter? Why bother even discussing this topic? Because the Bible says that *all* Scripture is profitable. That means we should seek proper understanding and interpretation because it will be profitable to us, even the difficult parts.

How I Found Out

Because I am not a theologian and I cannot cover the depth of this topic, I would like to first share with you the story of what happened to me. As I described at the start of this book, I had a crippling fear of the end of time. From the time I was a teenager until a couple years after I was married, the whole topic haunted me. I had nightmares about the Antichrist, bar codes (which I had been told were the "mark of the beast"), and constantly running for my life. I would wake up in the night and cry that God would save me. I wanted to escape so badly. The thought of ending my life had come to me more than once. I was terrified of the unknown.

If only I had understood earlier that knowledge is power! If only someone had told me! I think somewhere inside I knew I would have to face my fear in order to find out the real truth. I was sick and tired of people interpreting the Bible like an apocalyptic time bomb. In the end, I didn't care if there were a rapture or not. I just wanted the truth.

Early on in our marriage, someone directed me to a popular evangelist. I visited his website, as he was doing a series on End Times and had a prophecy timeline I could follow. I followed his chart for a while and it was apparent that according to his calculations, the Rapture was imminent! I felt a sigh of relief. Yet after only a few days of thinking about it, I felt I should do a little more research and make sure that the Rapture teaching was real. I remember coming across a few articles that seemed to blow away the arguments made for the Rapture. I was stunned. How could it be so easy to dismiss this rapture teaching that so many Christians believe? I was heavy-hearted again.

Within a month or so, the End Times topic came up when my dad was visiting. Since our family had experienced so much church drama and family drama over the years, theological debates did not surface often. Well, that night we had some company over and someone brought up the question of the Rapture. I was scared. I didn't know what my dad was going to say. I was afraid he might confirm my worst fears. For the record, my ultimate worst fear was that End Times prophecy would be fulfilled in my lifetime—just like I was told it would be—and that Christians would have to endure the torture and persecution of the Antichrist during the Great Tribulation and a one-world government set up by Satan.

I didn't realize at the time that this particular scenario, the no-rapture scenario that I grew up with, was a specific school of thought called "Historic Premillennialism." That sounds like a big term, but it simply means that they believe Jesus returns after a future Tribulation, but before the Millennium. I was so afraid of that scenario I couldn't even speak the words. As silly as it seems, I felt that if I spoke them aloud, it would somehow come true. It felt like I was in constant torture because of it. Somehow I had come to a disturbing conclusion. Looking back, I can summarize my fear and belief as this:

> Christ's death, resurrection, and ascension were for nothing. The Great Commission was a failure and will continue to be a failure. The Gospel did not spread throughout the world, and it *did* not and *will* not disciple nations. Satan is the literal god of this world. Satan will get the upper hand. Satan will rule and reign on this earth. Satan will slaughter the Church. Satan will continue to win battles on earth until the Church is defeated and he gets his one-world government. Satan will be victorious… at least until he is sentenced at the very end of history.

In a nutshell, that was my paralyzing belief. I didn't realize I believed all that, yet I had heard it preached from the pulpit in various subtle ways. I never heard a pastor say those exact words, but when they preached about future things that were going to take place, that is exactly the message that came across to me.

As we sat at the table with our company that night, I did my best to point out all the rapture indications I had learned that the Bible purportedly gives. I brought up the holy grail of rapture verses:

> *As it was in the days of Noah, so it will be at the coming of the Son of Man. For in the days before the Flood, people were eating and drinking, marrying and giving in marriage, up to the day Noah entered the ark; and they knew nothing about what would happen until the Flood came and took them all away. That is how it will be at the coming of the Son of Man. Two men will be in the field; one will be taken and the other left. Two women will be grinding with a hand mill; one will be taken and the other left.* (Matthew 24:37–41)

My dad pointed out, "The verse says that this event would be like the days of Noah. Read the verse again. In the event of the Flood, *who was taken away?* It wasn't God's people. It was the wicked! God took away the enemy and saved Noah and his family. The verse says 'They knew nothing about what would happen until the Flood came and took them all away.' This describes all those who rejected God and His warnings."

That blew me away. Never before had that verse made sense to me. Then he said something utterly shocking: "Well, did you know that there are other views besides a rapture or no-rapture view?" My immediate reaction was, "No, I did not! What do you mean? What other views?"

"Well there are people who don't believe all this prophecy was meant for a future audience. They believe that a lot of it was geared toward the Christians in the first century and much of it was fulfilled by A.D. 70 at the destruction of Jerusalem."

I believe my jaw was on the floor. A million more questions came to mind, but I remember something going "click" in my heart and mind. *Something* clicked. I had so many questions, but I knew I had just heard the truth. I immediately responded, "Wow… that makes so much sense!" I thought of so many other scriptures that had boggled my mind and suddenly made sense. For example, in Matthew 24, Jesus came out of the temple and His disciples ask Him three questions. "Tell us," they said, "when will this happen, and what will be the sign of your coming, and of the end of the age?" Jesus goes on to answer their questions and describes a host of what seems to us like cataclysmic and apocalyptic events. After He predicts all that is going to happen, He says this mind-blowing thing to His disciples in verse 34:

> *"I tell you the truth; this generation will certainly not pass away until all these things have happened."*

Well, that got me on a roll. I had to learn more. Of course, one of my first main questions was this: *Jesus said they would see the Son of Man coming in His kingdom before they would pass away, so... does that mean the Second Coming has already happened?* I learned soon enough that Jesus was using very dramatic Old Testament language His disciples would understand to describe a *judgment coming* on Jerusalem. I also learned the very phrase "Son of Man coming in His kingdom" has fuelled atheists in their schemes. They have often used the argument to try to disprove the Bible: "You see? Jesus said He would return in their own lifetimes and He didn't. Therefore, He was a liar and a false prophet, in which case we don't have to believe anything He says. In fact, if He were a liar or a false prophet, it means the entire Bible is based on a lie, which means Christianity is a false religion."

What would you say if an atheist used that argument on you? If you didn't know any better, they would have you right there! How many people have read this part of the Bible and been discouraged because they simply lack understanding of the real context? Context is key!

THE REST IS HISTORY

The next time I saw Dad, he handed me two books. The first one was *Last Days Madness*, by Gary DeMar. He said, "Read this. This will debunk all the myths you've believed." Then he handed me another one: *Paradise Restored*, by the late David Chilton. He said, "Here, after you read *Last Days Madness*, I want you to read Chilton. Gary's book will tear down the myths, and this book will build you back up."

You can guess what I did for the next few days. I could hardly put those books down. It was an interesting process because my fear had some very deep roots, like a bad weed. Sometimes as I would read Gary's book, the very suggestions in the chapter titles would give me waves of adrenaline. It took guts for me to read the whole thing, but I was so glad I did. He presented the historical errors that Christians have made in constantly predicting the end of the world, year after year, for centuries. They all had one thing in common: every single one of those predictions has been wrong! The only thing prediction-making ever does for Christianity is give unbelievers a foothold they can use to try to invalidate Christianity. Bad theology invalidates Christianity because it begins with a wrong premise and uses wrong assumptions that lead to wrong conclusions.

Those two books changed my life. After that, I couldn't stop reading and learning. I began to browse online Christian bookstores that offered different perspectives. I bought a Bible study DVD series called *Basic Training for Understanding Bible Prophecy*, and found it to be very simple and helpful. It walked through the entire chapter of Matthew 24 and a little of Revelation and Daniel. It taught me how to interpret the Bible for myself instead of relying on current events or modern prophecy teachers to decipher the codes for me. The series taught me that the way to interpret Scripture is by Scripture.

Whenever there is a word or phrase that is difficult to understand, the best way to understand it is to look at the way that word or phrase is used in other passages of Scripture. For example, when Jesus said, "This generation will not pass away until all these things take place," some people interpret the phrase "this generation" to mean the future generation that will see those signs. However, if we look at the way the Bible uses "this generation" in other parts of the New Testament, in every single case, you will find that "this generation" means *the generation that was being addressed*. Never in any single case does it mean a different generation. Some people will even go a step further and try to say that the word "generation" really means "race." We would then have to read Jesus' statement like this, "The Jewish race will not pass away until all these things take place." That doesn't make any sense at all. That would mean as soon as all those signs take place, the Jewish race would pass away.

The Scofield Reference Bible popularized both this and the newly-invented rapture theory around 1830. Historically speaking, dispensationalism—the fancy word for *Left Behind* theology—is a *new* theory, a theory that the church for many years threw out as heresy. It is now widely accepted in the modern church. This is why it's important to search out what we believe. We don't want to pass on bad theology anymore! We don't want to give our enemies the upper hand just because of our ignorance and failure to understand what the Word of God says.

Three Views

You need to know that there are different views about the end of time, the future, and who is really sitting on the throne. You need to know this because it will affect the rest of your theology. I will quickly explain the three main schools of thought and, very briefly, several variations within those views. It all centers on the question of the timing of Jesus' return and the beginning of the Millennium. It also centers on the question of whether or not the

Kingdom has been established yet, when that will be, and the repercussions of what that means. Here are the three main views within Christianity.

Premillennial View: In this view, Jesus returns *before* the Millennium, which is why you have the prefix *pre-*. The Millennium is a *literal* one thousand years. There are a few sub-groups within this view, which gets confusing. What you need to know is that, in general, the pre-millennial view teaches Jesus has *not* established His kingdom yet and that He is *not* reigning yet. This view holds that things will get worse and worse in the world, the Antichrist will set up *his* kingdom, and Jesus returns at the very end of time to rescue His nearly blotted-out church and usher in the Millennium. There are people within this group that believe the Rapture happens before the Tribulation, during the Tribulation, or after the Tribulation.

The famous *Left Behind* novels fit in this category under a specific title called "dispensationalism." This refers to the belief that the world is going to get really evil and bad, Jesus raptures His people just before the Tribulation, the Antichrist sets up his one-world government and then makes a covenant with the Jews, there is a rebuilt temple, and so forth. Jesus will physically rule from Jerusalem with military might and everything is distinctly Jewish. Dispensationalism makes the church separate from Israel. There are two peoples of God in this school of thought. This was around long before the *Left Behind* novels, but they popularized it all over the world today and you have most likely heard of them.

I cannot spend much time here debunking this theory, but I can assure you that the Bible speaks of no such thing as a rebuilt temple, or an Antichrist making and breaking a covenant with the Jews, an Antichrist setting himself up as a dictator ruling the world, etc. That is all very bad fiction, passed off as "literal Bible interpretation." I hope you will study this more and discover how very untruthful and unbiblical dispensationalism really is.

Amillennial View: This view means "no millennium." It says there won't be a literal Millennium of one thousand years, but the number "one thousand" is symbolic for a long period of time or a great amount, as in "God owns the cattle on a *thousand* hills." We know God owns the cattle on *all* the hills, but it is symbolic language used for making a point. Amillennialism holds that Christ has not *physically* established the Kingdom on earth, but the Kingdom is only *spiritual* in nature. The Millennium extends from the time Christ appears until the Second Coming.

This view holds that throughout time, there will be a growth of both good and evil. They will grow simultaneously together until God destroys evil at the end of time. In other words, the good will get better and evil will get worse. The Gospel will not conquer the earth, the nations will not be discipled, and Christ won't put His enemies under His feet. Any victory the Christian experiences is only in the spiritual. Increasing evil and lawlessness will overcome any Christian progress made on earth.

The problem here is that we have seen that the Bible says, "*The whole earth will be filled* with the knowledge of the Lord as the waters cover the sea." If this is true (and I have a tendency to believe God's Word), there isn't room for evil to be just as prominent a force as good. If the Great Commission is God's plan of redemption for history, and if the nations *will* be discipled, and if the yeast leavens the *whole* lump of dough, this means rebellion against God will become less and less influential in world affairs even as it becomes more and more concentrated. In addition, we know that Jesus has all authority in heaven and earth and that His kingdom is not of this world, but it extends throughout this world, in *all* realms, both visible and invisible.

Remember that if the Kingdom is only *spiritual* in nature, that leaves the physical realm to man (or Satan) to rule and reign as god. That leads us right back to this question: Who do you believe is sitting on the throne and ruling?

Postmillennial View: This is my personal view, the view from which I have written this entire book. This view holds that we are currently in the Millennium, which was established when Christ was here on earth. Like amillennialism, it agrees that the Millennium is not a literal one thousand years, but is symbolic for "a very long time." In fact, we might still be in the early church. This view says that the Millennium is a long period of slow growth where the world will convert to Christ. Jesus will return after He has made His enemies His footstool, after the Great Commission has been fulfilled in the world, and after the nations have been successfully discipled. This is a period of increasing worldwide prosperity and peace. Greg Bahnsen elaborates:

> There will be ups and downs, there will be times of persecution, there will be immorality and lawlessness to deal with. Nevertheless, the overall pattern will be that of growth and success for the kingdom. We will see prosperity in the church. It will grow through the gradual conversion of the nations—through the preaching of the Word of God—not through military might, not through guns and bazookas, but by the preaching of the gospel—the sword of the Spirit.[4]

We won't see total perfection here on earth, but things will definitely improve. Sin will not be gone either, but as people become more self-governed and restrain their carnal natures, submitting to Christ, sin will not be as rampant as it is now. We don't believe that every single person will be saved. There will always be wheat and tares; however, we will see an increase of Christianity and a decrease of all forms of rebellion.

Is this all just wishful thinking? While it certainly is the most optimistic of views, it doesn't matter if we think it sounds good or not. What matters is what the Bible actually teaches. We know the Kingdom is here now because Jesus said so in Matthew 12:28–29. "But if I cast out demons by the Spirit of God, the Kingdom has come upon you." Jesus cast out demons, so we know the Kingdom is here now, not in the distant future. Christ will return to His already established Kingdom to throw Satan into the pit and judge the world. The Resurrection and the Final Judgment are the same day.

Those are very briefly the three main views people hold about End Times and the future. We must be careful not to pick what just sounds good to us or what we've always believed. We must examine every idea and make sure it lines up with the Bible. I hope this opens your eyes to other views you may have never learned. I hope you are encouraged to read and study further the important questions of the future and what God has to say!

Chapter 15

Whence, Whither, Hither & To Whom?

No, this is not a chapter on Shakespeare or Old English Bible translations. We're going to look at some very pertinent questions that will help us determine where we're going in the future. We will consider these questions: For whom was Revelation written? To what events is it referring? What happens in the future?

I've told you the story of how I came to question my end times beliefs, and I shared some different views you may not have heard. Now I'd like to give you a little more meat to chew. I'd like to present one more piece of the puzzle in this picture of the future by showing you something about the past. I hope it will cause you to ask the questions it made me ask. I hope it will inspire you to dig even deeper and find out more about what the Bible really says concerning these matters, just as it did for me. Once you can put fear and hopelessness of the future behind you, there is absolutely nothing holding you back! You are officially "dangerous" to the devil.

An Important Piece of the Puzzle

As soon as I saw this single puzzle piece, everything started to make sense. The Bible was totally new and refreshing to me. It put all things into perspective. We've seen what God's plan is for the future and what He intends on doing with His kingdom: expanding and growing it until it fills the whole earth. So where does all this "Great Tribulation" and "Antichrist" stuff fit in? Let's take a very brief look at the context of when Revelation was written and to whom it was written. This will make you go, "Oh! I get it!" I'm going to make some general statements and then back them up with Scripture. There are entire volumes written on the approach I'm going to take, but I will merely sum it up here. If you desire to do more extensive research, I have listed some resources in "Further Reading."

John wrote the book of Revelation prior to the destruction of Jerusalem in A.D. 70. Some scholars think he wrote it later, but let me show you a couple of verses that support a pre-A.D. 70 position and let you decide. John is in the middle of receiving this vision when something happens to him:

> *Then I was given a measuring rod like a staff, and I was told, "Rise and measure the temple of God and the altar and those who worship there, but do not measure the court outside the temple; leave that out, for it is given over to the nations, and they will trample the holy city for forty-two months."* (Revelation 11:1–2)

The angel tells John to go and measure the temple—the Jewish temple—but not to measure the court outside. This tells us that the temple was *still standing* at the time of John's writing. The temple was destroyed in Jerusalem in A.D. 70, and that's how we know from Scripture itself that this vision came to John prior to its destruction. John couldn't go measure a destroyed temple. There would be nothing to measure. This bit of information fits in nicely with Matthew 24, when Jesus warns the disciples that within a generation (40 years), that this exact event would happen:

> *Jesus left the temple and was going away, when His disciples came to point out to Him the buildings of the temple. But He answered them, "You see all these, do you not? Truly, I say to you, there will not be left here one stone upon another that will not be thrown down."*

The account in Luke also echoes the verse in Revelation 11: "They will fall by the edge of the sword and be led captive among all nations, and Jerusalem will be trampled underfoot by the Gentiles" (Luke 21:24).

We also know that John recorded the Revelation during the reign of Nero Caesar. Again, the Scripture tells us here:

> *This calls for a mind with wisdom: the seven heads are seven mountains on which the woman is seated; they are also seven kings, five of whom have fallen, one is, the other has not yet come, and when he does come he must remain only a little while.* (Revelation 17:9–10)

Ken Gentry is an expert on the dating and context of the book of Revelation and explains really simply what this verse means and how we know Nero was ruling at the time:

> Perhaps no point is more obvious in Revelation than this: Rome is here symbolized by the seven mountains. After all, Rome is the only city in history universally recognized for its seven hills ....[1]

Gentry continues, giving incredible evidence from both inside and outside the Bible:

Whence, Whither, Hither & To Whom?

> John writes to be understood (Rev. 1:3) and specifically points out here that the wise one who follows the interpretive angel's declaration will understand: "This calls for a mind with wisdom. The seven heads are seven mountains on which the woman sits." (Rev. 17:9) . . . We learn further that the seven heads also represent a political situation in which five kings have fallen, the sixth is, and the seventh is yet to come and will remain but for a little while. Remarkably, we must note that Nero is the sixth emperor of Rome.[2]

We know from history the names of the seven emperors: Julius Caesar, then Augustus, Tiberius, Caius, Claudius, Nero, and Galba. The angel tells John that the first five kings are already dead, but the sixth one is still alive. That puts us at Nero Caesar. Nero died on June 9, A.D. 68. The angel says the seventh king had not come yet, and would remain only a little while. This is the Roman emperor Galba, who ended up reigning for only seven months—until January 15, A.D. 69. That's pretty amazing, don't you think?

There are huge books that delve into all the details on this, but I just wanted to show you quickly that Revelation was written before the destruction of Jerusalem, an event Jesus predicted would occur. This tells us a lot about John's audience—the Christians who were under persecution during the first century! Revelation is like much of the New Testament: it was a letter written to a specific group of people living at the time, addressing their current situation. Much of the Bible is written *to* specific people, but written *for* anyone who reads it, that they may benefit and profit from it.

Here is also how we know Revelation is written about the current events of the first century: The very first few verses in Revelation say the time of the predicted events were "soon to take place" and the time was "near." Take a look:

> *The revelation of Jesus Christ, which God gave him to show to His servants the things that **must soon take place**. He made it known by sending His angel to His servant John, who bore witness to the word of God and to the testimony of Jesus Christ, even to all that he saw. Blessed is the one who reads aloud the words of this prophecy, and blessed are those who hear, and who keep what is written in it, **for the time is near**.* (Revelation 1:1–3. Emphasis mine.)

John begins by saying what they are about to read concerns them because the time is near! "Near" does not mean 2,000 years in the future. "Soon to take place" does not mean anything other than "soon to take place." We always try to complicate everything, don't we? Somehow we have to make all this stuff in Revelation mean something that it doesn't. We say it's all about the future, and then twist it to fit our modern-day technologies, and it becomes a real mess—a real *fictional* mess. But as you know, fiction does sell.

Revelation closes with the same message with which it begins: the time is near for the first-century audience. The angel specifically tells John not to seal up the words of the prophecy book because of the fact that the events described were about to take place and the churches to which John was writing needed to be encouraged as well as informed.

> *Do not seal up the words of the prophecy of this book, for the time is near.* (Revelation 22:10)

This means that most of the events described in Revelation were all about the events leading up to and including the destruction of Jerusalem! That includes the Great Tribulation, in which John said he was a partaker (Rev. 1:9).

Does that make your head spin a little bit? When I saw that for myself, I thought, *Now that makes a whole lot of sense…*

This book only introduces some new ideas—well, ideas that might be new to us, but are, in fact, very old. This view has been in our church history for centuries. This message is all about hope, vision, and a reason to dig deeper and get off the theological milk we've been gulping! But *because* this is only an introduction, I will not be able to answer all the questions that arise about this topic. I hope you will look at the resources page I've provided for deeper study on these things.

Did You Know?

I should show you something now. This may surprise you. If you happen to be someone who has read all the popular *Left Behind* books and gotten caught up in the "rapture fever"—or maybe you just don't know what the Bible says—this an important piece of information to consider:

Did you know that the Book of Revelation does not even mention the word "Antichrist," not even once? There is a "beast" in Revelation, but they are two different things. If you're dying to know what the "beast" is and what "the number of the beast" means, it is similar to a Roman numeral equivalent of spelling out the name "Nero Caesar," except in Hebrew letters. The beast also represents the Roman Empire in general.

When you really get into these studies, you learn that most of the symbols and imagery are really Old Testament symbols and images. The New Testament wasn't compiled yet, so the first century Christians would have easily understood what all this meant since they were very well versed in the Old Testament.

We also have to remember there was great persecution in that day and John had to be discreet when sending this letter to those churches, so as not to cause them more trouble. That is why he said, "This calls for wisdom: let the one who has understanding calculate the number of the beast, for it is the number of a man, and his number is 666" (Rev. 13:18). He created a riddle for them. They would be able to figure it out just by transferring the number six hundred sixty-six to letters. Historical evidence indicates that this was a common game people would play in that time. John used it here so they would figure out what he was saying about Nero in the context of the persecuted Christian church. Nero was not a singular Antichrist figure. The Bible does not describe any such singular figure.

The only place the word antichrist is used is in John's epistles (1 John 2:18, 22, 23; 4:3; 2 John 7). Let's look at the Bible's qualifications of an antichrist. It's important that we don't put our own meaning into the text. John says an antichrist is anyone "who denies that Jesus is the Christ," or who "denies the Father and the Son," "every spirit that does not confess Jesus" and "those who do not acknowledge Jesus Christ as coming in the flesh. This is the deceiver and the antichrist." We can see very clearly here that an antichrist is not one individual. It is *anyone* who denies that Jesus has come in the flesh; hence, they are *anti-* (against) Christ. We also know that antichrist individuals were present at the time of John's writing because he says so. "And this is the spirit of the antichrist, which you have heard was coming, and is *now already in the world*" (1 John 4:3).

Instead of just reading the Bible and studying how the Bible uses terms and definitions, we have placed that authority in the hands of fiction authors and all those "experts." Guess what? The Bible is meant to be understood! The book of Revelation is called "Revelation" because it does not contain secrets and mysteries, instead it reveals them. It unveils a message. If you read it in its proper context, then everything really starts to make sense. Instead, "experts" have taken what would have made sense to first century Christians and forced it 2,000 years into the future! The Bible says an antichrist could be my neighbor or the Jehovah's Witness that knocks on my door, but for these end-times fiction authors, this is not nearly as exciting as a world political leader who will wipe Christians off the face of the earth.

Are there bad guys in the world who want to accomplish evil things like that? Yes, there are. There have always been bad guys who have wanted and tried to do that. This is nothing new. Just look at history. Go back to the Old Testament. Look at Rome. Look at all the horrid persecutions our Christian ancestors endured! We live in luxury compared to them. It may not stay that way for long if we keep thinking that some big bad Antichrist is supposed to rule the world! Do you understand why? Because if we really believe that Christ is not reigning over planet Earth, but the devil is, then we *expect* things to become more evil and we won't try to stop it, and because of that, we hand the world over to Satan on a silver platter!

Why It Matters

I bring up the end-times lies I believed because it affected my whole life. It affected my drive to live. It affected the decisions I made. Since I thought the world belonged to Satan and that it was supposed to get worse in order for Jesus to return, I had no plans to get involved and make it a better place.

There might be people who, after reading this, still believe Satan rules the earth, but who say they will try to make a difference in the world. I would challenge them to think about why. It is really a contradiction within that belief system. If things have to get very bad for Jesus to come back, then they should rejoice when they see atrocities committed in this world. Does that seem a little backward?

I know the enemy loves that kind of attitude. Since I had no hope for the future, I didn't have plans for the future. I didn't think about really wanting a family. It happened, but I didn't think about it and go, "Yeah, that's a really good idea." I also didn't have future generations in mind. I wasn't thinking about what the world might be like for my grandchildren if Christians like me didn't get involved… didn't commit to fulfilling the Great Commission. I had no plans to acquire assets or store up an inheritance for my future descendants, since I was convinced that none of us would be here due to the Rapture or the Tribulation. My beliefs on the end times had exponential effects in many ways. I'm still waking up to the realization of how much our beliefs about the future affect current and future generations that will, in turn, affect entire societies and civilizations. It is truly astounding.

If you are hearing some of this for the first time, it might be overwhelming. Maybe you have never thought about what you believed about these things. Maybe you have a blend of ideas and are confused. I would like to give hope to those who have struggled with fear and anxiety about the future. For those who think it does not matter what you believe, I would like to challenge you. What you believe about the future determines what you do today.

There is so much hope! I never understood what it was like to be free in Christ until I properly understood God's plan for the future of His church. I needed to get *that* to understand my own purpose and calling in life. If you don't know where you're going, you're going to just wander around and get lost. Purposelessness is something in which the devil rejoices. It is vital that we understand where we are going and how we'll get there.

CHAPTER 16

Return to Eden

If you just made it through the last few chapters, I'm giving you the proverbial high five right now. I know, that's lame. But honestly, I commend you for getting this far and bearing with me through some huge ideas. If this is all old news to you, then great! I'd like to add one last giant piece to the puzzle of the big picture for our lives. This was really the big *wow* factor for me when I learned this. It really made me see my significance in the world and my place in history.

Here's a statement you might have never heard: God's plan is to restore planet Earth to the pre-curse, pre-fall conditions before the end of time. The last thing He will destroy is death (at the very, very last day). In the meantime, God is working to restore the earth to Paradise—the pre-curse state of Eden before the Flood. Does that sound crazy or weird? I'm going to show you that this is true and is in the process of happening right now. Restoring the creation to pre-curse conditions has always been the theme of the Bible from Genesis to Revelation. This outcome will happen gradually, over a long period of time as the Kingdom permeates the whole world. It may take several hundred more years, maybe thousands. Yet, perhaps it is not so far away…

Much of this process involves our obedience and long-term commitment. That is why this truth is so exciting. The quicker we understand the biblical worldview of taking dominion in the earth and making disciples of all nations, the faster the curse will lift! This happens, of course, not through our own efforts, but through the power of the Holy Spirit. Jesus came to redeem the earth. When the Bible says, "For God so loved the world," the word "world" comes from the Greek word *kosmos*. *Kosmos*, usually spelled *cosmos*, means the whole created order. God so loved the entire created order that He sent His Son to die. Bulgarian writer Bojidar Marinov made an excellent point about this:

> We are saved not just to be saved. God has a higher purpose for us: Apply our deliverance and salvation to the whole creation. Does

that mean our social, political, and economic world as well? Yes. The verse says the *whole* creation.¹

Doesn't that give us a bigger picture? God is doing His work in the *kosmos* through us, His ambassadors. First, let's look at the state of the world according to Romans 8:18–22:

> *For I consider that the sufferings of this present time are not worth comparing with the glory that is to be revealed to us. For the creation waits with eager longing for the revealing of the sons of God. For the creation was subjected to futility, not willingly, but because of Him who subjected it, in hope that the creation itself will be set free from its bondage to corruption and obtain the freedom of the glory of the children of God. For we know that the whole creation has been groaning together in the pains of childbirth until now.*

The creation is waiting… for the lifting of the curse. The *kosmos* is groaning under the burden of this curse. Before the Flood, the earth was functioning in all its full glory. To what extent, we don't entirely know. Fossil records do show us that it was a tropical paradise all over the world, from pole to pole. We find palm trees and other tropical plants frozen in places like Antarctica, Greenland, and Alaska.

There are many theories within the Christian scientific community about this, but one theory is that before the Flood, a "water canopy" covered the earth, creating a "greenhouse effect." There is some debate on this theory, not because it isn't a biblical idea or a good explanation, but because we don't yet understand it all scientifically. We also can't explain why bumblebees are able to fly. Sometimes God defies our modern science. We have a long way to go still. One creationist science writer also pointed out this:

> Although the Bible does not specifically teach the canopy theory in so many words, there are several mysteries at least partially explained by it (the source of the waters for the 40-day rain producing the global flood, the longevity of the antediluvians, the lack of any rain before the Flood, the diurnal mist that watered the antediluvian lands, the origin of the rainbow, the greater size of most animal orders before the Flood, and others), that it can at least be offered as a good possibility. The scientific challenges are not insuperable. . . . What is wrong with simply believing what God has revealed in His Word, even when we don't yet have a scientific explanation for a particular problem? As the apostle Paul would say: "What if some did not believe? Shall their unbelief make the faith of God without effect? God forbid: yea, let God be true, but every man a liar . . ." (Romans 3:3–4).²

Our modern little vegetable greenhouses produce some of the same effects on a very small scale. They regulate the temperature throughout the space. It is always warm and the air is moist to give plants the ideal conditions to grow to their fullest. That is why before the Flood, everything was gigantic! Trees, bugs, and animals grew to unbelievable sizes. This is also why they had extremely long life spans. After the Flood, the earth's magnetic field changed, the altitudes changed, and the water canopy was gone. Now there was no water vapor cloud covering the earth, giving it the conditions for a warm, tropical paradise.

Could it be that this total change in altitude is why Noah got so drunk after the Flood? We know Noah was a man of character. It was the reason God saved him and his family. It certainly was out of character for him to sin in this way. After all, his family had been making wine for hundreds of years at this point. Why would he choose to get drunk now? That is strange. However, if you've ever talked to someone who has traveled to Switzerland and had one beer in a pub on a mountaintop, they will tell you all about the powerful effects of altitude change! This thought about Noah is not a fact, only a fun theory to ponder.

The point I'm making here is that the earth dramatically changed after the Flood. It was after the Flood that incredibly long lifespans began to decrease, but it happened slowly over several generations. People used to live as long as old trees! There will come a time when people will experience this type of longevity again. Isaiah prophesied what is to come before the Last Day:

> *"For behold, I create new heavens and a new earth;*
> *and the former things will not be remembered or come to mind.*
> *But be glad and rejoice forever in what I create;*
> *for behold, I create Jerusalem for rejoicing*
> *and her people for gladness.*
> *I will also rejoice in Jerusalem and be glad in My people;*
> *and there will no longer be heard in her*
> *the voice of weeping and the sound of crying.*
> *No longer will there be in it an infant who lives but a few days,*
> *or an old man who does not live out his days;*
> *for the youth will die at the age of one hundred*
> *and the one who does not reach the age of one hundred*
> *will be thought accursed.*
> *They will build houses and inhabit them;*
> *they will also plant vineyards and eat their fruit.*
> *they will not build and another inhabit,*
> *they will not plant and another eat;*
> *for as the lifetime of a tree, so will be the days of My people,*

> *and My chosen ones will wear out the work of their hands.*
> *They will not labor in vain, or bear children for calamity;*
> *for they are the offspring of those blessed by the* LORD,
> *and their descendants with them.*
>
> *It will also come to pass that before they call, I will answer; and while they are still speaking, I will hear. The wolf and the lamb will graze together, and the lion will eat straw like the ox; and dust will be the serpent's food. They will do no evil or harm in all My holy mountain,"* says the LORD. (Isaiah 65:17–25)

We know this is not about life in heaven because in this passage, there is still death. People are not dying at young ages, but very old ages. How exciting is that? It talks here about new heavens and a new earth. That can sound a little confusing at first, if we don't understand the whole context of the verse. We are actually in the new heavens and earth now: the New Covenant. "If any man is in Christ, he is a new creation; the old things have passed away; behold, all things have become new" (2 Cor. 5:17). We are all new creations when we are in Christ, and *all things* have become new. The old heavens and earth, so to speak, passed away when Jesus announced the Kingdom was here on earth. At His death, resurrection, and ascension, the New Covenant had begun. The phrase "new heavens and earth" is another way of saying "new creation." It is an Old Testament expression that is symbolic of God's creation under His Covenant (Isa. 51:15–20; Jer. 4:23–31). Gary DeMar writes:

> According to Isaiah himself, this "New Creation" cannot possibly be the eternal state, since it contains birth and death, building and planting (65:20–23). The "new heavens and earth" promised to the Church comprise the age of the New Covenant—the Gospel's triumph, when all mankind will come to bow down before the Lord (66:22–23). John Bray writes: "This passage is a grand description of the gospel age after Christ came in judgment in 70 A.D. and took away the old heavens and the old earth. We now have the new heavens and the new earth of the gospel age."[3]

The next verse describes a New Jerusalem. This does not mean ethnic Jerusalem, but represents the Church in the New Covenant. There is only one people of God now, not two. There is only one Jerusalem, which is the Church as a whole. The late David Chilton clarified this:

> John next saw "the Holy City, New Jerusalem, coming down out of heaven from God, made ready as a Bride adorned for her Husband" (Rev. 21:2). No, it's not a space station. It is something which should be much more thrilling: it is the Church. The Bride

is not just *in* the City; the Bride *is* the City (cf. Rev. 21:9–10). We are in the New Jerusalem now. Proof? The Bible categorically tells us: "You have come to Mount Zion and to the City of the living God, the heavenly Jerusalem, and to myriads of angels, to the general assembly and Church of the firstborn who are enrolled in heaven . . ." (Heb. 12:22–23; cf. Gal. 4:26; Rev. 3:12). The New Jerusalem is a present reality; it is said to be coming down from heaven because the origin of the Church is heavenly. We have been "born from above" (John 3:3) and are now citizens of the Heavenly City (Eph. 2:19; Phil. 3:20).[4]

THE END OF ANTI-WRINKLE CREAM

This incredible passage goes on to describe a time within the New Covenant (the new creation) where there will be a lack of sorrow and strife. There will be fewer miscarriages and infant deaths. If you die at a hundred years old, you will be considered accursed and a mere youth! It says God's people will have the lifespan of an old tree, just like the pre-flood conditions. It is interesting to observe how our lifespans have already increased considerably in the last century. Because of good sources of food, clean water, proper hygiene, and medical treatments, life expectancy has significantly risen and continues to rise. You hear more and more these days of folks living well over one hundred and even competing in marathons! The gospel gives us the science and technology to increase our lifespan in those ways.

All our modern medicine came from Christians who applied the Bible in science, knowing one must start with the right premise for things to work and for science to advance. But beyond the efforts of man, there is a spiritual aspect that goes on in the longevity of life: freedom from sin. Sin is the whole reason death exists, and why we have short lifespans from the start. It is the curse.

As new creations in Christ, we are still born into sin, but we are no longer slaves to sin. When we return to the Law of God and when we meditate on it day and night (Psalm 1), the result will be self-governance and self-restraint. We have already seen the incredible domino effects of an individual who practices self-government.

The key to the return of long lifespans is the return to God's Law. When you have a Christian nation that practices self-government, it means they are not slaves to their sinful nature. That means the effects of sin are not as present. It means the effects of freedom in Christ are present: spiritually and physically, internally and externally. When Romans 8 says the earth is groaning and waiting for the sons of God to be revealed, this indicates that the sons of God *will* be revealed eventually. This also implies there is an aspect of personal response and action in faith.

We must restrain our sin, individually and collectively as a nation, in order to see this lifting of the curse. It has already begun. It will continue to unfold as the years pass and as we commit to love God and obey His commands.

Verse 21 says there will be a time when God's people will enjoy the fruit of their labor. Instead of working so hard and never seeing the fruit of that labor, or experiencing the slavery of heavy taxes, we will get to enjoy our work. We will get to keep our work and keep our income. I believe this indicates the civil government will return to the laws of God, deflate to the small size it should be, and govern in such a way that does not interfere with profit and production. Remember that according to God in 1 Samuel, anything over ten percent is considered tyranny and puts people in slavery. Because of this, I think it is a reasonable expectation that as the Kingdom of God grows and permeates the whole world, taxes will decrease to lower than ten percent, where we are no longer in financial bondage to our civil government.

Verse 22 says we will wear out the work of our hands, but that it won't be in vain. Make no mistake: we will be working hard. This is not some utopian retirement village. God created man to work. From the day God formed Adam, he worked in the garden. He named animals; he beautified the garden and exercised his dominion over the earth. We are in the will of God when we work hard and delight in our calling.

Vegetarianism is "In"

The passage goes on to say the Lord will bless God's people—and their children. This is going to be a multi-generational time of blessing and prosperity. The last verse describes a pre-curse type of condition where wolf and lamb graze together. Here is another passage in Isaiah that describes this same future state:

> *The wolf shall dwell with the lamb, and the leopard shall lie down with the young goat, and the calf and the lion and the fattened calf together; and a little child shall lead them. The cow and the bear shall graze; their young shall lie down together; and the lion shall eat straw like the ox. The nursing child shall play over the hole of the cobra, and the weaned child shall put his hand on the adder's den. They shall not hurt or destroy in all my holy mountain; for the earth shall be full of the knowledge of the* Lord *as the waters cover the sea.* (Isaiah 11:6–9)

Animals go back to being vegetarians, as they were in the Garden of Eden. How very interesting, don't you think? Chilton makes another important point here about how all of this is contingent on our obedience:

> On the other hand, God warned, the Curse would reappear if the people turned away from God's Law: "I will let loose among you the beasts of the field, which shall bereave you of your children and destroy your cattle and reduce your number so that your roads lie deserted" (Lev. 26:22; cf. Num. 21:6; Deut. 28:26; 2 Kings 2:24; 17:25; Ezek. 5:17; 14:15; 32:4; Rev. 6:8). When a culture departs from God, He surrenders its people to the dominion of wild animals, in order to prevent them from having ungodly dominion over the earth. But in a godly culture this threat against life and property will progressively disappear; and, ultimately, when the knowledge of God shall cover the earth, the animals will be tamed, and harnessed again to the service of God's Kingdom.[5]

Now when you compare all of this with Romans 8 where it says, "The creation itself also will be set free from its slavery to corruption into the freedom of the glory of the children of God," I think it is an incredible parallel! The creation itself will also be set free. People are not the only ones being set free in Christ. It's the whole *kosmos*. The creation itself will be liberated from its bondage to the curse and will be given to us, the children of God, to exercise dominion over it just as God had originally designed for us to do in Eden. The meek will inherit the earth (Ps. 37:11, Matt. 5:5). This does not mean we will be free of sin or that there will be no unbelievers in the world. It just means that in a general way, the church will be so dedicated to their love for God and in fulfilling His commands, that they will not be slaves to their sinful natures, which will bring about great prosperity. Cornelius Van Til spoke clearly about this:

> Redemptive revelation of God had to be as comprehensive as the sweep of sin. Redemption must, in the nature of the case, be for the whole world. This does not mean that it must save every individual sinner in the world. It does mean, however, that the created universe which has been created as a unit must also be saved as a unit.[6]

How comprehensive was the sweep of sin? It got everywhere. There is nowhere on earth it did not touch. That is also how comprehensive redemption will be! This also means Christianity will so influence the world that even unbelievers will live peaceably under God's authority.

Remember when Jesus told the parable of the mustard seed? The tiny seed grew into a tree and the birds of the air came and took refuge in it.

The tree is the church. When it has grown so big and influential because it is functioning properly and faithfully, the whole world will look to it for refuge and answers. The church will become a place of comfort and answers for the world. This is the Kingdom of God that has successfully discipled the nations. This is what dominion is all about. This passage in Ezekiel also mirrors Isaiah:

> *Thus says the* LORD GOD, *"On the day that I cleanse you from all your iniquities, I will cause the cities to be inhabited, and the waste places will be rebuilt. And the desolate land will be cultivated instead of being a desolation in the sight of all who passed by. And they will say, 'This desolate land has become like the Garden of Eden; and the waste, desolate, and ruined cities are fortified and inhabited.' Then the nations that are left round about you will know that I, the* LORD, *have rebuilt the ruined places and planted that which was desolate; I, the* LORD, *have spoken and will do it."* (Ezekiel 36:33–36)

There again, we see what God's intentions and plans are. He is the rebuilder of nations. We are the workers. It is not Christians who bring all this about, it is the work of the Holy Spirit through us. "I the LORD have spoken and will do it." God will make all this happen. We respond in obedience and do the work. He blesses us. We teach our children to do the same, to take dominion, to have an explicitly biblical worldview, and to go into all the world and make disciples of the nations. This is how the whole world is going to change.

OBEDIENCE OR LAW OF ATTRACTION?

We hear a lot these days about how God wants to prosper us financially. This is generally true. The imbalance has come through what is called "the prosperity gospel," or the popular message of "health and wealth." This message preaches that it is *always* God's will for *every* believer to be prosperous and healthy *all the time*; that if you just have enough faith, you can acquire riches and be free of physical ailments. This is not true. This is what I call a Christian version of the popular New Age book called *The Secret*. *The Secret* is a philosophy that Oprah popularized on her show and now everyone is talking about it. It's a best-selling book and DVD. It promotes the idea of what they call "the law of attraction." The law of attraction says that if you just think about things hard enough and believe hard enough, you can have all the desires of your heart. It is very appealing to the carnal nature. The only mention of God is the new age god, described as "light" or a "source" or whatever suits your fancy. It ultimately speaks of that god as a sort of Santa Claus. You just send positive thoughts out into the universe, have "faith," and then the universe will bring you what you want. The prosperity gospel is dangerously close to this. It substitutes some of the terms with more Christian-sounding words, but the theology is essentially the same. Guess what? The God of the Bible does not work that way! Sometimes we ask God for things and He says, "No!"

Now, generally speaking, God really does want His people to prosper financially and physically, but sometimes He clearly has other plans for His people. Sometimes there are real times of chastisement and cursing. Sometimes it is simply failure on our part to obey His commands. Sometimes it is actually part of God's divine plan when people are not well. "The LORD said to him, 'Who gave human beings their mouths? Who makes them deaf or mute? Who gives them sight or makes them blind? Is it not I, the LORD?'" (Exod. 4:11). It's clear from this verse that God declares His sovereign purposes over both the healthy and the sick.

We can take great comfort in this. Does God want us to pray for people to be healed and recover? Yes, He does. Sometimes He has other plans though. We can be assured that it is all bringing Him glory in one way or another, only we are so short-sighted we cannot see the big picture. When God chooses not to heal someone of their sickness, it is not because they didn't pray hard enough or didn't believe God could do it. Sometimes it's simply because it is the will of our sovereign Lord. We have to accept that. Oftentimes God really does answer our prayers and choose to heal people, and we rejoice in it.

You can also read the story of Job and see very clearly that God allowed Satan to test Him in horrific ways. Job is not the only believer who has gone through terrible times in life! Was Job in the will of God? Yes, he was! Was he obedient? Yes! Did Job not have enough faith? Job had *great* faith, which is why he never cursed God! The apostle Paul faced amazing trials and afflictions, despite his faith and godliness. He wrote,

> *Five times I received from the Jews the forty lashes minus one. Three times I was beaten with rods, once I was pelted with stones, three times I was shipwrecked, I spent a night and a day in the open sea, I have been constantly on the move. I have been in danger from rivers, in danger from bandits, in danger from my fellow Jews, in danger from Gentiles; in danger in the city, in danger in the country, in danger at sea; and in danger from false believers. I have labored and toiled and have often gone without sleep; I have known hunger and thirst and have often gone without food; I have been cold and naked.* (2 Corinthians 11:24–27)

Was Paul in the will of God? Yes! Was he obedient? Yes! Did Paul just not have enough faith? Paul had *great* faith, which is why he was able to endure what he did and continue in his ministry. So while it is generally true that God does want to prosper His people and have them free of disease and suffering, there certainly are times when we go through what seems to be "disfavor," and it is all a part of His divine plan. Sometimes the trials are there to test us. Sometimes the trials are there to chastise us and rebuke us when we have been sinful. There are certainly times in history when a nation rebels against God and receives the obvious consequence that rejection of God brings, which is destruction and judgment. There certainly are times when we just don't understand why things are happening the way they are. Every single believer seems to experience this at one time or another. We may rest in knowing this: "All things work together for good to those who love God, to those who are the called according to His purpose" (Rom. 8:28).

In light of these scriptures and observations, I'd like to point out some of God's strategies of the eventual transfer of wealth from the wicked to the righteous:

> *Evil people may have piles of money and may store away mounds of clothing. But the righteous will wear that clothing, and the innocent will divide that money.* (Job 27:16–17)

> *To the person who pleases Him, God gives wisdom, knowledge, and happiness, but to the sinner He gives the task of gathering and storing up wealth to hand it over to the one who pleases God.* (Ecclesiastes 2:26)

> *A good person leaves an inheritance for their children's children, but a sinner's wealth is stored up for the righteous.* (Proverbs 13:22)

> *Whoever multiplies his wealth by interest and usury gathers it for him who is generous to the poor.* (Proverbs 28:8)

We have to look at these scriptures in light of the overall plan God has for church history. It is not a "think positive and get rich" theology. It is God's strategy to deliver the earth into our hands when we are mature enough to handle it—when we have demonstrated we will commit to His way of doing things.

If we don't submit to God's Law, to God's system of economy, to God's worldview, to God's education, to God's plan for every part of life, we will not inherit the earth! This is a classic promise that is contingent on our obedience. God grants us the ability to obey, and we have to take action and do it.

We have nothing but hope and joy to expect. When I first learned these truths and saw it in the Bible for myself, I was blown away! It sure puts changing diapers into perspective, if you ask me. When you expect a bright future and have the motivation to obey because you know there are promises for you and your children, it really makes you take joy in the present, mundane tasks of life. It makes hard work worth it, knowing it's not all for nothing. We are not working in vain, but for a real future. It could be a while until we see this kind of freedom on the earth, but, with every new person who digs deeper into the Word to find out what God has in store for His people, it may not take as long as we think!

CHAPTER 17

Seven Questions

I want to use this chapter to ask seven questions (as the chapter title would suggest), and to these questions I will give my own answers. But I challenge you to consider these questions for yourself and take the time soon to formulate your own responses.

1. *What do you really believe about the Great Commission?*

My answer: The Great Commission will be a success in history, not a failure. We will successfully go throughout the world and make disciples of all nations. Christ will return when He has made every enemy His footstool. If you believe in the Rapture and a particular Antichrist figure who rebuilds a temple and makes a covenant with the Jews and rules the world for seven years, you really believe in the defeat of Christianity. You believe that what Christ set out to do did not work. You believe the Great Commission will not disciple all nations and that Christ will not be returning for a glorious Bride. You believe in the slaughtered Bride. That is a dangerous belief. If you are still confused or want to study this further, please see the resources page. Our family will know where Satan rightfully belongs: under our feet... and not because we have power in ourselves, but because we are empowered by the Holy Spirit. God fights for us. We obey.

2. *What kind of impact has the church's negative view of eschatology (or what we call "End Times") had on the world?*

My answer: Because the church has joyfully accepted a theology of defeat, it has also retreated from involvement in the world and neglected positions of authority and dominion. This has resulted in the increase of non-Christians in those positions. Where Christians step down, pagans step up. We even see the effect of this glorification of Satan's power and undermining of Christ's power in pop culture and films. If you browse your local video rental store there are dozens of thriller and horror movies all about End Time scenarios, antichrists, and apocalyptic end-of-the-world films. It is really mockery. Even if the filmmakers don't know it, it mocks God because it tries to depict a God who is impersonal and impotent in history. Satan always wins. Satan is God's equal and has just as much authority as God. The End Time scenarios show God as a loser in history and Satan as triumphant. Cataclysmic, end-of-the-world films show God as uninvolved in the affairs of man and that asteroids, giant earthquakes, and natural disasters are out of His control.

This is all mockery. Mockery has seeped out of the church and into society. What is going on outside the church is a reflection of what is going on inside the church (or the lack of what should be happening inside the church). This mockery of God is on us. This is our fault. We have to take responsibility for dropping the ball. We accepted the idea that Satan has authority here on earth, that Jesus does not have all authority in heaven and earth, and that Satan will conquer the church in history. It's time to pick up the ball again. It's time to set a new course. Remember: *if the church doesn't change the culture, the culture will change the church.*

3. *What do you really believe about the power of Jesus?*

My answer: Is Jesus a loser in history? Is He not so powerful that He can't overcome His enemy with one look? If you believe He can, if you believe the Great Commission will be fulfilled, if you believe the earth will be filled with the knowledge of the Lord, if you believe that the rock will become a mountain that fills the whole earth as portrayed in Daniel 2, then you are a postmillennialist! You believe Christ will return on the Last Day to receive His glorious Bride, not a Bride that looks like she was a victim of a chainsaw massacre. If you believe the Bible when it says Jesus will return after He has made all His enemies His footstool, then you cannot have a pessimistic view of the church, believing the church will either decrease in power, or evil will grow at the same rate as Christianity. If Christianity is permeating the world, evil cannot be doing likewise. There is only one winner. God has predestined this battle. Sorry, Satan, but this game is already rigged. You lose. As David Chilton so eloquently put it:

> The eschatology of dominion is not some comfortable doctrine that the world is getting "better and better" in an abstract, automatic sense. Nor is it a doctrine of protection against national judgment and desolation. To the contrary, the eschatology of dominion is a guarantee of judgment. It teaches that world history is judgment, a series of judgments leading up to the Final Judgment. At every moment, God is watching over His world, assessing and evaluating our response to His Word. He shakes the nations back and forth in the sieve of history, sifting out the worthless chaff and blowing it away, until nothing is left but His

pure wheat. The choice before any nation is not pluralism. The choice is obedience or destruction.[1]

4. *What will happen if the people return to loving the Lord by obeying His commands?*

My answer: Ultimately, the nations will be discipled. Jesus said, "If you love me, you will obey my commands" (John 14:15). The proof is in the pudding. If individuals return to obeying the Ten Commandments, applying those commandments in all of society, teaching them to their families and children, giving the world real working answers to real-world problems, the nations will be discipled. The world will be full of the knowledge of the Lord as the waters cover the sea.

5. *How are you changing the course of history right now?*

My answer: One diaper at a time! Be faithful in the small things. They add up to a lifetime of influence. We only have one shot to get this right. We have one chance to show God our complete love and submission to Him. This is so far beyond a gushy feeling for God or an emotional experience. This means action. It means having a good attitude on what feels like the worst day (which is a big challenge). It means refusing to let the government disciple your kids. It means teaching the Ten Commandments as the standard in our homes and holding ourselves accountable to it. It means giving ourselves a kick in the behind when we know we have been nagging our husbands or withholding intimacy from them as a form of manipulation. It means equipping ourselves with godly discipline methods that the Bible commands, not what pop psychology recommends. It means loving our kids and our neighbors even when we don't feel like it—because God first loved us. Be faithful in the small stuff. It will ripple out all around you.

6. *How are you thinking about the near future and the long-term future?*

My answer: I anticipate the spreading of Christ's victorious Kingdom here on earth. He will accomplish this through families. I am actively planning my daily activities and attitudes with multi-generational victory in mind. Our family will assess the current times and plan for them accordingly (economic collapse, market instability, etc.). We will also have a long-term plan in mind. Every move we make is a step toward this long-term plan. For fun, my husband and I have talked about acquiring enough wealth that we could start a Christian film company that makes huge, epic films of Bible stories and historical Christian biographies. We envision *Lord of the Rings*-style theatrics and production. It would draw all kinds of people who may or may not realize it is a Bible story or Christian account, but would share the message of God's sovereignty and power over history. It's fun to plan and dream of doing things like that!

7. *What kind of impact can the Church really have in society?*

My answer: The church is to be a city on a hill. It is to be salt. It is to give flavor to a bland world and it is to preserve the culture by teaching them to obey God's commands. The church is to be that mustard seed that grows into a tree and all the birds come to rest in it. The church is to be a refuge. It is to have real, working solutions to poverty and unemployment.

The Bible has specific blueprints for how the church should take care of the poor. Handing out free money is not taking care of the poor. The Bible says, "The one who is unwilling to work shall not eat" (2 Thess. 3:10). The solution to poverty is putting all able-bodied people to work.

George Grant has written a most inspiring book on the subject called *Bringing in the Sheaves*. I will tell you one thing: I never felt passionate about helping the poor until I read this book. This book made me want to jump up and do something. He provides a real, biblical blueprint for how we are to help the poor—and it works! It is not just a theory, it's a practical handbook he has successfully used in his own community for years.

Helping the poor is not about making them more comfortable in their poverty, it means equipping them with the motivation, the skills and education necessary to work their way out of poverty and teach others to do the same. This is from the biblical model God gave us in the Old Testament called "gleaning." God instructed farmers to leave the outer edges of their fields and crops for the poor, the widows and orphans, and for travelers passing through. They had to go harvest it themselves, which was often very labor-intensive, but the reward was that they could eat that day.

The Bible shows us a working example of this in the book of Ruth. This is an important point: welfare is not the government's job. It is the church's job. The government has done a terrible job of "ending poverty" and instead of doing that, it has created *more* poverty. People have become dependent on the government to take care of them. After all, why should someone get a minimum wage job when they can just fill out a form and get paid for doing nothing? It's much easier. How should Christians think about government policies that support programs and welfare? George Grant makes an excellent point:

> The reason for Western prosperity is not accidental. It is the direct outgrowth of the "Puritan ethic" which involved diligent labor, saving, investment, and the philosophy of free enterprise and initiative. God's Law clearly promises external blessings in response to external obedience. Work is that external obedience. In his seminal work entitled *Idols for Destruction*, Herbert Schlossberg states, "Christians ought not to support any policy toward the poor that does not seek to have them occupy the same high plane of useful existence that all of us are to exemplify. 'Serving the poor' is a euphemism for destroying the poor unless it includes with it the intention of seeing the poor begin to serve others." Whereas humanitarian social policy keeps people helplessly dependent, Biblical charity seeks to remove them from that status and return them to productive capacity. Biblical charity seeks to put them back to work because Biblical charity should never be anything other than a prod to full restoration of the poor to their God-ordained calling. Paul makes it plain: "If a man will not work, he shall not eat" (2 Thess. 3:10). A handout does not charity make! Every effort must be made to ensure that our helping really does help. A handout may meet an immediate need, but how does it contribute to the ultimate goal of setting the recipient aright? How does it prepare him for the job market? How does it equip him for the future? How well does it communicate the Law of God and the precepts of Biblical morality?[2]

While the world system promotes laziness, God's system promotes productiveness and purpose. There really are people who are in need and are not lazy, but there is a far better solution for them. Remember what God calls a society that wants their government to take care of them? A society of slaves. They are in bondage. When the government takes care of you, you have forfeited personal responsibility, and you are now a slave. The fact that government is doing what the church is supposed to be doing is an act of tyranny. It has crossed over the boundary of the sphere God created for civil government and gone into the sphere of the church's work.

The problem is that the church doesn't seem to be too willing to take up this challenge. We give money to the food bank, but do we have a real biblical plan of action for putting local people to work? Are we opening our homes and discipling the homeless of our town? Are we educating them and ministering to their souls as well as their stomachs?

Unless we give the homeless and hurting a real hope in Jesus Christ, they will remain in spiritual poverty first, and secondly, they will have no real reason to work towards something better. It is the hope of the gospel permeating the whole world that gives us the motivation to work hard. It is the dominion mandate that commands us to work and take care of ourselves and the domain God gives us.

I can barely touch on this subject, but I want to suggest one more idea that is exciting. If the church is really functioning biblically as outlined in Scripture, it will revolutionize the nations. George Grant addresses this point in his book and I highly recommend reading it for further study.

If every church were to take care of their own congregation (the widows, the orphans, the single moms and dads, and their own elderly members), *and* they sponsored *one* poverty-stricken family outside the church—and every church did this—we could completely eliminate the entire welfare system altogether!

This is not going above and beyond what God requires; this is simply following what God commands. We are to take care of our own. We don't send them to the government to get help. We equip them, serve them and help them help themselves. There are requirements and contingencies that God has outlined in Scripture so that people won't take God's mercy for granted. They have to meet certain standards and have a good attitude. They have to be willing to get out of their current position. If they are content being miserable in poverty, they do not qualify. That is God's standard, not ours.

As I said before, George Grant has a whole book written all about this amazing biblical blueprint God has given us. I hope you are inspired to get a copy, give it to your pastor, and start promoting God's solutions to our world's problems!

CHAPTER 18

The Ultimate Legacy

Now that we have a grasp of both the past and the future of the Kingdom, we have a much better idea of what we should be doing right now! This part gets me really fired up and excited because I love practical stuff. I think most moms do. Here is a whole chapter on what we should actually *do* with all this knowledge.

We are working toward building a significant inheritance for our children, spiritually, theologically and, Lord willing, financially too. This is all a part of the expanding of the Kingdom. *Legacy* is part of dominion.

Here in southern British Columbia, Canada, it is extremely difficult for a middle class, working family to buy a house. Our taxes are very high and the cost of living is very high. Unless we are born into wealth or a family member gives us a large sum of money, many families will not own property.

The reason God takes private ownership seriously is because it teaches us stewardship. It increases our maturity and level of personal responsibility. It is also a big step in getting out of the world's system—which doesn't want you to own anything—and brings us closer to independence. The more independent we can be from the system of the world, the world's economy and dependence upon it, the better off we will be.

Say you own your own land, your house is mortgage-free, you have a large vegetable garden, and you've built or converted your house to self-sustainable methods of heat and power. You are now officially "off the grid." If one day God decided to judge our nation to the point that everything collapses, your family would have no problem thriving in the midst of chaos.

The bottom line is that we want to prepare for whatever God has planned for our nation: both judgment and victory. Judgment is inevitable. We have it coming, and we've had it coming for a long time. We've disowned the God who made us the most prosperous nation in the history of the world. We sacrifice our children every day, killing them by the thousands in the name of "choice," or giving them over to Pharaoh so he can have his way with their minds. We still have human sacrifice in our society. We also say we hate the devil, but we sure love his economic system and don't think twice about it. We have gone off "hard" currency and replaced it with fake currency. So now, our whole society runs on a system of fraud and theft. We have an education system that teaches the religion of secular humanism under the guise of "neutrality," all paid for by the citizens of the country. We are paying to secularize our nation. Through high taxes, we rob each other and pay for our children to learn to ignore God, hate God, and worship the State.

Do you think God will continue to allow these abominations? I believe we are in an early time of judgment now. What we have seen thus far with the economic collapse may only be Episode 1 of God's justice. It is not the work of the devil. It is the work of God rebuking the devil and all who follow his ways. Do you think that God should spare His people when they have been happy to get in line and follow the world's system? Why should He save us from His judgment when we have been part of the scheme that is slapping God in the face?

We don't deserve to escape it. If God decides to show us grace and mercy in this situation, we will see our sin. We will understand and grasp the conspiracy that has been going on all along since the Fall: to thwart God's power and dominion on earth and replace it with a counterfeit system and a counterfeit god.

When we finally "get it," we will spend our every waking moment fighting it, getting off the treadmill of the world's system, and getting on God's system. We have to get out of this rat race. This is going to involve planning. This is going to involve creativity. Besides doing the things I've already mentioned like changing your attitude about your feminine role and influence, making it your life's mission to have a biblical worldview, getting your kids out of Pharaoh's boot camp (public school), and learning to discern the times—besides all that—we are going to start planning on building something. We will rebuild what the devil has destroyed. We will build up an inheritance for our children, both spiritually and financially.

Author Joel McDurmon gave a lecture on protecting our wealth from the hands of the enemy and I took careful notes that I will share with you now. There is an important reason for doing these things: it teaches self-government (which we know has an incredible domino effect) and sets up the next generation for success and dominion.

1. Invest in understanding.

Until we educate ourselves in what it is that God wants us to do differently from the world, we remain Satan's useful idiots. Consider this piece of wisdom:

The Ultimate Legacy

> *I walked by the field of a lazy person,*
> *the vineyard of one with no common sense.*
> *I saw that it was overgrown with nettles.*
> *It was covered with weeds,*
> *and its walls were broken down.*
> *Then, as I looked and thought about it,*
> *I learned this lesson:*
> *A little extra sleep, a little more slumber,*
> *a little folding of the hands to rest—*
> *then poverty will pounce on you like a bandit;*
> *scarcity will attack you like an armed robber.* (Proverbs 24:34)

So while the world's tactic is to covet something, then devise a scheme, and then act in robbing (like high taxes and borrowing), this scripture says we need to see what the world is doing, reflect on it, and then receive instruction: don't do what the world is doing!

2. We need an emergency plan in place.

We need money: at least a six-month cash reserve and some cash on hand. Buy a good safe and bolt it down somewhere. While investing in gold and silver is a good thing to do because it's God's money (and we will work to see it back in our money system), in an emergency situation, you will need cash.

Food: two to three months of non-perishable items. If you have a garden, that is great. Don't forget water. You can use all these things on a regular basis, but replenish them every time you go shopping so that the items don't expire.

Supplies: medicine (homeopathic remedies don't expire) and first aid kits. Don't forget toilet paper and shampoo. Camping gear would be useful as well.

3. Diversify your income.

Create multiple sources of income. For example, Abraham had different kinds of cattle, silver, gold, and servants. Don't put all your eggs in one basket. If the market crashes in one industry, you don't want to be left hanging. There are plenty of home-based businesses that allow you to work the hours you want and that have high commissions and bonuses. Business expert Robert Kiyosaki, the author of *Rich Dad, Poor Dad*, has written a book called *The Business of the 21st Century* on how network marketing is a great option for people who don't have a lot of money to start a business. It gives them the opportunity to profit the most by creating "passive income." This is one of many options worth considering.

4. Strengthen community relationships.

During hard times, you don't want to be all on your own. Relationships are what will get you through difficult times and give you the support you need to press on and encourage one another. Tight-knit communities will do just fine during times of economic collapse because they have built trust with their family, their church, their neighbors, and outside networks.

5. Beat inflation.

Remember, inflation means that the government is injecting fake money into circulation to make it appear as though we have more than is really there. What that does is causes each dollar to be worth less. It has less purchasing power. That is why prices have to increase. High prices make up for the lack of actual money that is there. Until we change the whole mentality of our government, we can rest assured that they will continue to inject money into circulation. This means prices will continue to rise. It's called a "boom/bust" cycle. If we want to beat inflation, we need to buy what we need now as far as supplies go. Buy property now if you are able, instead of renting. Invest right now in real estate, become a property owner (landlord) if you are able, and acquire real, hard currency like gold and other hard assets such as guns and ammunition.

I am not a financial advisor; I am only making suggestions to help us get off the treadmill of the world's system and get on to God's program. We want out of slavery! We also want our children to succeed us. We want them to surpass us and go far beyond the borders we approach. This is all a part of generational planning.

In old Europe, families built estates over the span of several generations. A family worked from the ground up, acquired land and passed it on to their children. Instead of selling the land, their children built a house and planted gardens. They passed what they had built on to their children. Those children acquired the skills and knowledge of their parents and grandparents, became entrepreneurs, and improved the land, house, and garden. They continued to add value and growth to the family land until it became a very wealthy estate. The original owners did not get to see the end result, but they had the privilege of beginning a family dynasty. This shows great faith that we do not have over here.

Think of the great cathedrals over in Europe. Some of them took hundreds of years to build. How were they able to keep the vision and pass that vision on to the next generation? They found a way to implement a generational legacy within their children so that they would finish the task their parents started.

This is an unbelievable concept here in Canada and the U.S. Here, we build houses and churches with cheap materials that may last only one generation. We think very short term. With the prevailing end-of-the-world mentality our church and society has, why would we build things to last? We see fewer family businesses now as well. Here in America, it's every man for himself. It seems that even when a family has a successful business, the children want to be "independent" and "find their own way." They have no family vision for a lasting business. I'm not saying they shouldn't apply their skills in ways other than the family business, only that there is such a lack of family vision and family dynasty.

One amazing example of a father who had a long-term vision for his family dynasty was a man named Arthur Guinness. In 1759, he founded the Guinness brewery in Ireland. He took out a lease on the land for 9,000 years. Now that was a man with vision! Arthur's descendants continued in the family business until 1992! This kind of hard work and family legacy is inspiring.

Another interesting note is that the Islamic religion has a 100-year plan. They mean to take over the world within a specific time frame. They are serious about it. They privately educate their children, making sure their children properly adopt their worldview. They are catechizing them in the ways of their false religion, which is hostile to Christianity. We must realize that every family catechizes their children whether they mean to or not. It's either intentional or unintentional, but it is happening. What is striking is that even these Muslims are smart enough to keep their children out of the government schools. They know what is at stake: the minds of their children. They also have many children. They don't abort them at the rates we do. They often build family businesses and you see families dwelling together as they slowly gain influence and power in our country. They are strategic. Christians today are not. What do you think will happen in one to two generations if we don't change things right now?

If the enemies of Christ are plotting 100-year plans, I think Christians should have 200-year plans. We need to look into the enemy's camp, see what they are up to, and then fight it with a better strategy. Let's go further than they do. I once watched a conference on DVD about the idea of a 200-year plan for Christian families. It really inspired my husband and me to think long-term in ways we had not before. I will highlight here some of my notes from one session.

Developing a 200-year plan

The world approaches the future like this: "The best way to predict the future is to create it." The world thinks it can just manipulate the present and the future however it decides. The world thinks it can create its own destiny. That is a false ideology.

The Christian approach to the future looks like this: "Who considers the power of your anger, and your wrath according to the fear of you? So teach us to number our days that we may get a heart of wisdom" (Ps. 90:11–12).

We are the creatures, not the Creator. We do not control the future, only God does. In fearing God, we need to number our days. We realize we have a limited amount of time on this earth. We should not waste God's time and spend it idly or foolishly, pursuing our own selfish ambitions that have nothing to do with the kingdom or passing on a legacy to our descendants. When you get life insurance, they can make a rough prediction, based on your health and lifestyle, when you will die. Of course, God could take us out anytime He likes, but if He gives us long life, we can roughly predict how long we have to accomplish what we hope to accomplish for the Kingdom while we're here on earth.

We number our days so that God may grant us a heart of wisdom: wisdom to know what to do with those days. The whole idea is to formulate a tentative plan of Kingdom work here and then present it to the Lord. "Commit your work to the Lord, and your plans will be established" (Prov. 16:3). Our entire life's mission should be to instill a theological legacy to help our children and grandchildren to become leaders, seekers of the Kingdom, defenders of the faith, ambassadors of Christ, warriors, reformers, and spokesmen of the Gospel who can stand in the gates and not be ashamed. We have to teach them how to define those terms and apply them in today's generation.

Families need to create their own unique mission statement. When we have a family mission statement—a real mission statement that declares what this family's objective is in the world and how we're going to carry it out—it gives children a sense of belonging and purpose. It gives them hope and a charge in the world. We might go after a specific sphere perhaps—like reforming the art and music in our culture, or perhaps science or psychology—and draft up a rough timeline as to how and where we seek to influence and make changes, and by what date we hope to accomplish those goals. It is a flexible plan that can be changed and amended in time with wisdom. Having something like this is wonderful for our descendants. They will never have to wonder, *What was it that our original patriarch hoped to accomplish?* It gives us priorities both locally and internationally. When we talk of expanding the Kingdom, this extends not just to our own community but also across the globe. Maybe your family's mission will be to cultivate a culture that embraces the Law of God in a foreign country.

Write letters to your children and future descendants. This is essentially what I'm doing in this book. While it is my intention to share the knowledge God has brought to me in the last few years to anyone willing to receive it, it is also for my children and future descendants. Should something happen to my husband and me, they will have this book and understand first hand, *Oh! That's what Mom and Dad were all about! We will carry this torch for them and pass it on to our children's children.*

I suggest you do the same. It doesn't have to be a book. It could be a series of short letters. Keep them somewhere safe. Tell them about the little things that bring you joy, to the things you love about your husband, and the hope God has put in you for the future. Tell them what you have learned about marriage and give advice as to how to find the right mate. Outline your suggestions and experiences. You never know when you will no longer have the chance to do so. What a treasure it will be for your family to have such wisdom passed on!

My last point for long-term vision is that we need to have the optimism and fierceness of Saint Patrick of Ireland. He originally had a different name, but adopted the name "Patrick" when he later became a priest. He was born in A.D. 389, during the time of the Roman Empire's decay.

If you think times are bad now, just read history books to find out how awful and nasty it was during that time. It was utter chaos. Disease and plague, war, heavy taxation, rampant sexual immorality, and even the language was being displaced. As a boy, Patrick was living with his family in Britain when he was kidnapped and taken to Ireland. Sold as a slave, Patrick herded pigs on a farm for six years. There he was, living as a slave in a foreign country where he didn't even know the language! Times were not good. It was here he witnessed the pagan culture of Druidism, witchcraft, and idolatry.

The Lord saved him at some point during all this. Patrick recorded his recognition of God's sovereignty over his life, despite the terrible things he was going through:

> The Lord brought me to a sense of my unbelief, that I might, even at a late season, call my sins to remembrance, and turn with all my heart to the Lord my God, who regarded my low estate, and, taking pity on my youth and ignorance, guarded me, before I understood anything, or had learned to discern good from evil . . .[1]

When God saved him, he became a real prayer warrior. He prayed night and day. He prayed without ceasing! One day, Patrick ended up escaping and managed to get on a ship. During the voyage, a storm blew in and he ended up in France. It was there he joined a monastery. Years later, he had an important dream. He recorded it in his account called *Confessions*:

> I saw in a vision of the night a man whose name was Victoricius, coming as if from Ireland with innumerable letters, one of which he handed to me ... and while I was reading aloud the beginning of the letter, I thought at that very moment I heard the voice of those who were near the Wood of Foclud, which is by the Western Sea, and they cried out thus as if with one voice, "We entreat thee, holy youth, to come and walk still among us." And I was very much pricked to the heart, and could read no more, and so awoke.[2]

So finally, at age 40, during the year 432, Patrick and twelve other monks crossed the dangerous winter sea back to Ireland. By this time, the Barbarians were pillaging Europe. Times were frightening. Patrick and the monks went back to look for his old master. They found out he had been killed by a neighboring tribe. If Patrick had not escaped on the ship when he did, surely he would have been killed too. God continued to reveal His providence to them.

The next bold move they made was to go to the hall of a Druid lord who was feasting there with his Druid priests and warriors. One of their messengers ran into the feasting hall and announced the arrival of these strangers. The monks entered the dark, smoky hall carrying a giant cross. The Druids were all dumbfounded. Then Patrick began to preach to them in their own tongue, which he had learned while he was a slave. This alarmed them and caused them to be defensive at first.

Can you imagine their surprise? The Druid chieftain was amazed and not only granted them religious tolerance in the land, but was also baptized! He then donated the land for their first church!

After that, there was a lot of Druid opposition and it put Patrick in much danger. He was almost killed twelve times and was once kidnapped (again) for two weeks.

Despite all the attempts on his life, God demonstrated through this one humble servant that He was more powerful than all the magic and paganism of the last few thousand years. During Patrick's time in Ireland, many Druid chieftains converted, along with their tribes.

Patrick used simple imagery to explain complex theological concepts. He allegedly used the three-leaf clover to explain the Trinity, which is why it is traditionally associated with Ireland. Patrick discipled people and left ministers everywhere he went. He founded over 300 churches and baptized over 120,000 converts. Before he died, he wrote:

> But I pray those who believe in and fear God, whoever may think fit to look into or recieve this writing which I, Patrick, a sinner and unlearned, wrote in Ireland, that no one may ever say, if I have demonstrated anything, however weak, according to the will of God, that it was my ignorance [which produced something noteworthy]. But do you judge, and let it be most firmly believed, that it was the gift of God. And this is my Confession, before I shall die.[3]

The saying goes that Patrick found Ireland pagan, and left it Christian. It is also because of the Christian Irish monks and scribes that we have any records of world history and literature, including our Bible. When the Barbarians invaded Europe, they burned everything they could get their hands on, but incredibly, and providentially, the Irish monks preserved these documents. Author and Irish historian Thomas Cahill wrote:

> Patrick's gift to the Irish was his Christianity—the first de-Romanized Christianity in human history, a Christianity without the socio-political baggage of the Greco-Roman world, a Christianity that completely inculturated itself into the Irish scene. Through the Edict of Milan, which had legalized the new religion in 313 and made it the new emperor's pet, Christianity had been received into Rome, not Rome into Christianity! Roman culture was little altered by the exchange, and it is arguable that Christianity lost much of its distinctiveness. But in the Patrician exchange, Ireland, lacking the power and implacable traditions of Rome, had been received into Christianity, which transformed Ireland into Something New, something never seen before—a Christian culture, where slavery and human sacrifice became unthinkable, and warfare, though impossible for humans to eradicate, diminished markedly.[4]

The life of Saint Patrick inspires me. In the midst of terror, chaos, and great opposition, he was faithful in the small things. He faithfully persevered, praying every day and committing his every breath to the purposes of God—and look at what God accomplished through him! He turned an entire island from paganism in one lifetime! Think about that. One man in one lifetime with the hope and optimism in the midst of dark days prayed that the Gospel would conquer and win the hearts of the nations.

How many Christians do we have in the world today? Millions! Imagine what would happen if we mobilized our faith and actually did something! We've made our salvation all about us. We've limited the scope of the gospel to me, myself, and I. It's all about us and our own little lives. We've become totally self-centered and focused on how our Christianity can benefit us. It's all about if we got something out of the worship service. It's all about if we are "getting fed." The late R. J. Rushdoony articulated this thought even further:

> Too often, the modern theologian and churchman goes to the Bible seeking insight, not orders. Indeed, I may go to Calvin, Luther, Augustine, and others, to scholars Christian and non-Christian, for insights, for data, and for learned studies, but when I go to the Bible I must go to hear God's marching orders for my life. I cannot treat the Bible as a devotional manual designed to give me peace of mind or a "higher plane" of living; it is a command book which can disturb my peace with its orders, and it tells me that I can only find peace in obeying the Almighty. The Bible is not an inspirational book for my personal edification, nor a book of beautiful thoughts and insights for my pleasure. It is the word of the sovereign and Almighty God: I must hear and obey, I must believe and be faithful, because God requires it. I am His property, and His absolute possession. There can be nothing better than that.[5]

While we do find joy and satisfaction in our service to the King, it is not all about what we get out of it. It's about the big picture of what God is doing in history. This moment is nothing. Somehow, God orchestrates all these nothing moments into something over time, that results in His ultimate purpose for the *kosmos*.

It will take the courage and boldness of Saint Patrick to truly commit to the long-term permeation of the gospel in all nations, but it is the most important, purposeful, and attainable cause that we could ever aspire to. It will happen.

Wives and moms are a central part of history making and culture changing. Changing diapers has never been fun, and I really hate that it takes seventeen steps to complete one load of laundry. But with a Kingdom vision in mind, a victorious eschatology, a biblical worldview to equip me, and children to share in the legacy, I'm all for doing these house chores. They are the most important Kingdom tasks we could ever take on!

CONCLUSION

I Found the Puzzle Box!

Do you remember in the beginning I described how many of us have a 5,000 piece puzzle spread all over the table, but we've lost the box with the picture on it? Well, we have finally come to the place where we will try to view this big picture in full and see if we can make any sense of the pieces.

I hope by now you have seen a glimpse of the glorious hope we have in Christ and the bright future to which we look forward. We have a high calling, filled with promises, contingent on our obedience.

We've looked at how our thinking on the future can affect the now. We have seen the impact of what a real purpose and calling in life can do. It brings deep significance and meaning into doing the family's dishes and cleaning up that special "finger painting" project in the baby's crib.

It also brings incredible meaning in martyrdom if that is the case. This is the hope our Christian ancestors carried with them. It is the reason they were so willing to die: they knew the gospel would prevail. Sacrifices are inevitable. We do not believe that everything is going to be just peachy and wonderful from here on out. We know there is a war—and sometimes wars get really ugly. But because we know who wins and who will gain continual victory, we can be assured that the sacrifice is not for nothing.

The discipline we had to give our kids day-in and day-out was all working toward something: shaping warriors for the future battles of generations.

We looked at how important a biblical worldview is for moms who want to change the world—not just for that reason, but also because God commands us to have the mind of Christ. The outworking of this is cultural change. We briefly saw the importance of discerning the times, planning, preparing and getting familiar with what's really going on in the world. We looked at some terms and popular beliefs we have about our government. We learned that God has His own world order and divine objective. Our goal should be to get off the treadmill of the world's system and get onto God's system as soon as possible. We also examined some popular beliefs about End Times and the future. I wish I could cover more on that topic, but the bottom line is that I am not an expert and it would take a whole book to go through it thoroughly. There are far better resources for that and I am happy to recommend them.

If you feel inspired by any of this, you will obviously want your husband on board. You can encourage him in these ideas, just as Queen Esther did. Make sure you approach him with respect and his favorite dish, and I'm sure he will be open to hearing what you have to say.

I have plenty of resource suggestions that he can look into if he wishes to get well-respected men's views on these issues. I only condensed all these big ideas into one small book because wives and moms are busy and often don't have the time or patience to plow through all those thick books, although if you can, it is really worth it.

In the meantime, I pray you will pass this message on to those you know. They need the true hope of the gospel.

The world is hurting out there, and we Christians are hurting in here. It's hard to help the world when we're limping ourselves.

I pray you will take comfort in your role at home with your husband and kids. I pray you will understand the gravity of your position, that you are changing the course of history in one way or another, either intentionally or unintentionally. I pray you will make it your life's mission to live with a Kingdom purpose in mind in all things.

We are God's weapon for victory.

When the world's system fails, when it collapses and decays, we will be here to reconstruct it… from the bottom up… one diaper at a time.

ENDNOTES

Chapter 4

[1] Matthew Henry, *Commentary on the Whole Bible*, 1 vol. (Peabody, MA: Hendrickson Publishers Inc., 1991), 12.

Chapter 5

[1] Michael Specter, "THE BABY BUST: A special report.; Population Implosion Worries a Graying Europe," *The New York Times Online*. Published July 10, 1998.

http://www.nytimes.com/1998/07/10/world/the-baby-bust-a-special-report-population-implosion-worries-a-graying-europe.html?pagewanted=all&src=pm
Accessed 01/20/12.

[2] Specter, "THE BABY BUST."

[3] Specter, "THE BABY BUST."

[4] Voddie Baucham, "Is an Economic Downturn A Good Reason to Stop Having Kids?", *Voddie Baucham Ministries Blog*. Published June 11, 2009.

http://web.me.com/voddieb/vbm/Blog/Entries/2009/6/11_Is_An_Economic_Downturn_A_Good_Reason_to_Stop_Having_Kids.html
Accessed 01/20/12.

[5] "The Top 100 Reasons Not to Have Kids (and Remain Childfree)," *Childfreedom Blog*. Published March 17, 2009.

http://childfreedom.blogspot.com/2009/03/top-100-reasons-not-to-have-kids-and.html
Accessed 01/20/12

Chapter 6

[1] Kelly Crawford, "We Need More Arrows," *Generation Cedar Blog*. Published June 16, 2008.

http://www.generationcedar.com/main/2008/06/we-need-more-arrows.html
Accessed 01/20/12

[2] Dennis Peacock, "How to Build a Christian Worldview," seven-part audio lecture by Strategic Christian Services.

Chapter 7

[1] Gary DeMar, "Legalism, the Mosaic Law, and the New Testament," *American Vision: Articles*. Published January 19, 2010.

http://americanvision.org/1600/legalism-mosaic-law-testament/
Accessed 01/20/12.

Chapter 8

[1] Noah Webster, *American Dictionary of the English Language*, 1828.
  http://www.1828-dictionary.com/d/search/word,educate
  Accessed 01/20/12.

[2] Andrew J. Coulson, "The Real Cost of Public Schools," *The Washington Post Online*. Published April 6, 2008.
  http://www.washingtonpost.com/wp-dyn/content/article/2008/04/04/AR2008040402921.html
  Accessed 01/20/12.

[3] Webster, *American Dictionary*.
  http://www.1828-dictionary.com/d/search/word,presuppose
  Accessed 01/20/12.

[4] See Samuel Blumenfeld, *Is Public Education Necessary?* (Powder Springs, GA: American Vision Press, 2011).

[5] Charles Francis Potter, *Humanism: A New Religion* (New York: Simon and Schuster, 1930), 128.

Chapter 9

[1] *"Macho Man" Mark Driscoll* [Video]. (2007). Retrieved 01/20/12 from
  http://www.youtube.com/watch?v=fSrZVF3FEUQ

[2] *Todd Friel explains the gospel* [Video]. (2010). Retrieved 01/20/12 from
  http://www.youtube.com/watch?v=FY6CXOAIsTc

Chapter 10

[1] R. J. Rushdoony, "Problems," *California Farmer,* 240:7 (Apr. 6, 1974), 35.
  http://chalcedon.edu/research/articles/problems/
  Accessed 01/20/12.

Chapter 13

[1] Gary DeMar, "Fellow-Partakers in the Tribulation and Kingdom," *American Vision: Articles*. Published April 10, 2007.
  http://americanvision.org/1717/fellowpartakers-tribulation-kingdom/
  Accessed 01/20/12.

[2] Sarah Phillips, "Stage II: Mixing and Kneading" of "Stages of Yeast Bread," *Baking911.com*. © 2000.

http://baking911.com/learn/baked-goods/bread/stages-yeast-bread/stage-ii-mixing-and-kneading
Accessed 01/20/12.

CHAPTER 14

[1] R. J. Rushdoony, "Eschatology," *Journal of Christian Reconstruction*, Symposium on Eschatology, Vol. XV: Winter, 1998, p. 11.

[2] David Chilton, *Paradise Restored* (Tyler, TX: Dominion Press, 1994), 8–9.

[3] Greg Bahnsen, *Victory in Jesus* (Texarcana, AR: Covenant Media Press: 1999), 3.

[4] Bahnsen, *Victory in Jesus*, 27.

CHAPTER 15

[1] Kenneth, Gentry, *Navigating the Book of Revelation*, (Fountain Inn, SC: Goodbirth Ministries, 2010), 20–21.

[2] Gentry, *Navigating the Book of Revelation*, 20–21.

CHAPTER 16

[1] Bojidar Marinov, "The True Gospel vs. the Truncated 'Gospel,'" *American Vision: Articles*. Published February 9, 2011.

http://americanvision.org/4020/the-true-gospel-vs-the-truncated-gospel/
Accessed 01/23/12.

[2] Henry Morris, Ph. D., "Let the Word of God Be True," *Institute for Creation Research: Articles*.

http://www.icr.org/article/let-word-god-be-true/
Accessed 01/23/12.

[3] Gary DeMar, "What Does Peter Mean by the Passing Away of Heaven and Earth? A Study of 2 Peter 3," *American Vision: Articles*. Published October 11, 2010.

http://americanvision.org/3603/what-does-peter-mean-by-the-passing-away-of-heaven-and-earth-a-study-of-2-peter-3/
Accessed 01/23/12.

[4] Chilton, *Paradise Restored*, 205.

[5] Chilton, *Paradise Restored*, 205.

[6] Cornelius Van Til, *An Introduction to Systematic Theology* (Phillipsburg, NJ: Presbyterian & Reformed Publisher, 1974), 133.

Chapter 17

[1] Chilton, *Paradise Restored*, 220.

[2] George Grant, *Bringing in the Sheaves* (Atlanta, GA: American Vision Press, 1985), 78–79.

Chapter 18

[1] St. Patrick, *The Confession of St. Patrick*, trans. Rev. Thomas Olden (Dublin: James McGlashan, 1853), 44.

[2] St. Patrick, *Confession*, 57–58.

[3] St. Patrick, *Confession*, 77–78.

[4] Thomas Cahill, *How the Irish Saved Civilization* (New York: Random House, 1996), 148.

[5] R. J. Rushdoony, *God's Plan for Victory* (Vallecito, CA: Ross House, 1982), 69.

FURTHER READING

Apologetics

Basic Training for Defending the Faith
  by Greg Bahnsen (DVD), American Vision

Defending the Christian Worldview Against All Opposition
  by Greg Bahnsen (Audio), American Vision

Collision (Douglas Wilson vs. Christopher Hitchens)
  (DVD), American Vision

God Is: How Christianity Explains Everything
  by Douglas Wilson

Kingdom of the Cults
  by Walter Martin

Christian Worldview/Theology

How to Build a Christian Worldview
  by Dennis Peacock (Audio), Strategic Christian Services

By This Standard
  by Greg Bahnsen

75 Bible Questions Your Instructors Pray You Won't Ask
  by Gary North

Amazing Grace: The History and Theology of Calvinism (DVD)

Church/Family

Divided (DVD),
  National Center for Family Integrated Church

Family Driven Faith
  by Voddie Baucham

The 200 Year Plan: A Practicum on Multi-Generational Faithfulness
  (Audio), Vision Forum

Building a Family that will Stand
  (Audio), Vision Forum

Culture

Bringing in the Sheaves
  by George Grant

Liberating Planet Earth
  by Gary North

Unconditional Surrender
  by Gary North

Return of the Daughters
  (DVD), Vision Forum

Demographic Winter
  (DVD), Vision Forum

Education

The Children of Caesar
  (DVD), Voddie Baucham Ministries

The Children Trap
  by Robert Thoburn & Gary North

Whoever Controls the Schools Rules the World
  by Gary DeMar

End Times/Eschatology

Basic Training for Understanding Bible Prophecy
  (DVD), American Vision

The Book of Revelation Made Easy
  by Kenneth Gentry

Last Days Madness
  by Gary DeMar

Paradise Restored
  by David Chilton

Late Great Planet Church
  (DVD), Nicene Council

Politics/Economics

Agenda: Grinding Down America
  (DVD), American Vision

Socialism: A Clear and Present Danger
  (DVD), Vision Forum

God and Government
  by Gary DeMar

How to Argue with a Liberal… And Win
  edited by Joel McDurmon

Where to Find These Materials and More

AmericanVision.org

NiceneCouncil.com

VisionForumMinistries.org

NCFIC.org

Chalcedon.edu

KennethGentry.com

CONNECT WITH THE AUTHOR

Facebook: https://www.facebook.com/DiapersDishesDominion

Blog: http://www.DiapersForDominion.com